GOODBYE, AMERICAN DREAM?

GOODBYE, AMERICAN DREAM?
How We Got Here and What To Do About It

AARON JAFFE
with MARDA DUNSKY

HAPPY WARRIOR PRESS
Evanston, Illinois

Happy Warrior Press
Copyright © 2012 Aaron Jaffe, Marda Dunsky
All rights reserved

Library of Congress Control Number: 2012930945

ISBN 978-0-9851779-0-4

www.GoodbyeAmericanDream.info

Printed in the United States of America

*For my wife, Charlotte,
who has been my partner
in achieving our own American dream*

*For my parents, Karl and Dora,
who taught me that the American dream was possible
for myself, my children and my grandchildren*

*And for all those today
who stir us to believe
that the American dream is worth fighting for*

CONTENTS

Acknowledgments
ix

1. An American Worldview
   1

2. A Politics Not of the People
   27

3. No Easy Way Out
   73

4. Not So Easy Listening
   127

5. Goodbye, American Dream?
   167

Notes
222

ACKNOWLEDGMENTS

The life of our country, like our own personal lives, goes through cycles.

Today the United States is experiencing a cycle in which fear and doubt prevail to a degree not seen in decades. Americans are losing faith in their government and are starting to believe that they are helpless to change things for the better.

I do not believe that we are helpless. We can turn things around. In order to do so, the American people must counter malaise with an open and honest national conversation about the issues that confront us today. Then we must unite and act.

My purpose in writing this book is to contribute to that conversation and to encourage that action based on my 42-year career in public service. As I began to gather my ideas in the summer of 2010, I realized that what's at stake in our current national predicament is nothing less than the American dream.

This book would not have come to fruition were it not for my co-author, Marda Dunsky. A skilled writer and researcher, she helped me develop and articulate my ideas. She kept us moving forward and shaped our work through a series of revisions.

At various stages of those revisions, we called on people whose opinions we valued to review our work. Their notes were invaluable and helped guide – and in some cases, correct – our thinking. For their time and consideration, I would like to thank Judge Martin Ashman, John Betancur, John Fischer, Michael Holewinski, Richard Longworth, Mufid Qassoum and Glenn Schneider.

I am also grateful to Deborah Leigh Wood and Richard Phillips for their editing assistance.

Last but certainly not least, I want to thank my wife, Charlotte, and my children and grandchildren, whose support and encouragement for this endeavor inspired me.

Aaron Jaffe
February 2012

GOODBYE, AMERICAN DREAM?

1
An American Worldview

I was born in 1930 to immigrant Jewish parents on the West Side of Chicago. My father, Karl, had come to the United States as a young man from Poland after World War I; my mother, Dora, from her native Lithuania. I grew up with my two older brothers, Nate and Marc, in the Lawndale neighborhood near the crossroads of Roosevelt and Pulaski.

It was the depths of the Great Depression. The year after I was born, the idea of "the American dream" was reborn – popularized in 1931 by historian James Truslow Adams in his book *The Epic of America*. As many Americans were going through the hardest times they had ever known, amid economic turmoil and social dislocation, Adams gave us what became, for decades to follow, a hallmark of American optimism and a metaphor for the American spirit:

> [T]he American dream, that dream of a land in which life should be better and richer and fuller for every man, with opportunity for each according to ability or achievement.
> ... It is not a dream of motor cars and high wages merely, but a dream of social order in which each man and each woman shall be able to attain to the fullest stature of which they are innately capable, and be recognized by others for what they are, regardless of the fortuitous circumstances of birth or position.[1]

At home and on the streets of Lawndale, my parents and their fellow immigrants didn't talk about the American dream using those words. But they had the same idea when they would say: We came to America for a better life.

Their circumstances in Europe had been difficult, and even though they were facing hard economic times in their new land, they felt that here, they were free. So many things were possible; people could move up. My father would tell me: "I'm laying the foundation for you, so you can build the first floor and rise in society. Your children will build the second floor, and so on."

Although times were hard, I grew up with this sense of possibility, and it has been central to my "happy warrior" optimism – the feeling I have had throughout my life that everything will turn out all right. But this sense has been shaken by the circumstances that we are facing today as a result of what has been dubbed the Great Recession.

People are losing their houses, they're out of work, they have no health insurance. So many of the problems that we overcame in the decades following the Great Depression have resurfaced, albeit in lesser magnitude, since the Great Recession began in late 2007.

It seems that we have been thrown back to the past. Until recently the trials people faced during the 1930s had vanished in the decades that followed. Americans went back to work and rocketed to the moon, and our country achieved a degree of prosperity, along with technological advancements and military might, that would have been unimaginable when I was growing up.

But today we have lost ground. Our troubles are palpable, their manifestations increasingly apparent. They have percolated to the surface of our present reality, and my own iteration of these concerns now finds its way to these pages. In search of answers, I offer a glimpse backward to better understand a way forward.

The Lawndale of my youth was a primarily Jewish neighborhood and also somewhat Catholic. In some ways, the Jews who came over from the old country didn't leave the old country behind. They belonged to *landsmanschaften*, groups whose members hailed from the same regions in Europe, and from these they organized *vereins*, or social clubs. But whatever these immigrants' origins, most were delighted to be in America. They loved this country because they saw in it opportunity and possibility that they knew they would not find anywhere else in the world.

My father came from a town in Poland that appears on the map as *Wysokie Mazowieckie*, which he pronounced as "Wysoker Mazevetzky." His people came to America leaving oppression behind. They had not been permitted to be part of the larger society. They lived in *shtetls*, segregated towns populated mostly by Jews. There were many professions that Jews couldn't practice and for which they were denied access to education.

These new Americans referred to the United States as "the golden land." They thought that anyone could make it here – and they knew they hadn't come here only for themselves. They came for their families, for their children. They wanted their children to grow up in a society where they could be free and have the good things in life. Where they could think freely, talk freely and worship freely without retribution from the predominant culture.

My father never talked about the hard life he left behind, but my mother would, on occasion, refer to her life in the old country. Dora had lived through pogroms in Lithuania and would tell stories about how a chicken had saved her life. "One day I bent down to pick up a chicken," she would say, "and a bullet went over my head."

In my home today hangs a photo of her brother's wedding in 1913 or 1914. All those in it would perish in the

Holocaust except my mother. I grew up hearing stories about her town in Europe, and I always felt that if somehow I were to be transported there, I would know everyone.

My father, Karl, was a tailor. He came to America as a young man and he went to work. He put his pennies together and eventually was able to bring his mother and several brothers and sisters over from the old country. My father worked two jobs. He had a little shop of his own, the Karl Jaffe Tailor Shop on Pulaski Road, where he did tailoring and pressing and sent dry cleaning out to a factory.

During the fall and winter he also worked in a women's coat factory – this when such manufacturers existed in Chicago. He did piecework and was paid per garment. There was no such thing as minimum wage, and his earnings were minimal.

My father never went on "relief" – as government assistance was called in those days – but we were pretty far down the economic food chain. Living through the Depression, though, I didn't think of myself as poor. We always had food on the table, and my father the tailor could always fix me up with a pair of pants.

As a child I lived in a building where each apartment was heated by a stove – but this was a land where you could advance from living with stove heat to living in an apartment heated by steam from radiators.

My father owned an apartment building, but he lost it during the Depression. It had six units, all stove heat. Many of the tenants couldn't afford to pay the rent and seldom did. If they needed food, though, my mother would bring it over.

To the average Jewish family, going on relief was considered a *shanda*, which meant a shame or scandal. It was a sign that you were a greenhorn who couldn't make it here. But it was the Depression, and many people had no choice but to go on relief. Work was seen differently then from how it is seen today: Almost every job was a noble job. If you were able to work and had a job, that was wonderful, with a few exceptions.

For example, in our community, actors were not thought of as working or as having jobs, but as *luftmenschen* – people who lived on the air. My father never told me that Sam Jaffe, who played the title role in the 1939 epic *Gunga Din*, was a relation; this I learned from a cousin. My father would say: "Butcher, plumber, ditch digger – *those* are jobs. But if you're an actor, what do you contribute to society?"

Contributing to society through work and education were important values in our family and community. When you worked, you provided for your family. And when you did that, your children could get an education. Instead of being a tailor, maybe your kid could become a teacher or doctor or accountant and could advance. The thing that let you advance wasn't the money but the education.

However, education was considered an extremely important means to social mobility. If you had a car, you could lose it; if you had an education, no one could take that away from you. You could do something with your education so that you could get another car.

The idea was to become part of the mainstream. With money you could live a better life, but with an education you could do more for society, and that was your responsibility. Because education was far more important than money, it wasn't a question of whether I could or would go to college. I was going to college, period, because education was the bottom line.

Back then, higher education was affordable. I went to the University of Illinois and UCLA and then attended law school at DePaul University. Tuition cost a couple hundred dollars a semester, not the fortune that it costs today. This made higher education accessible to most people, providing race or religion didn't get in the way at universities that had quota systems. Those barriers have largely disappeared, but today they have been replaced by economic barriers that have the same effect of excluding people.

When I was growing up, many people were out of work and having a rough time. But we helped one another. We learned that you are your brother's keeper.

If your friend was hungry, you were supposed to help him, not judge him. It wasn't that he was a bum because he was hungry – maybe he had lost his job or was ill. My mother and father helped people even though we were not wealthy. If Mrs. Hyson next door was sick, my mother would walk over there with food.

It was like praying in the synagogue: A traditional congregation couldn't start its prayers until it had the 10th man for the *minyan*, or quorum. We lived next door to a synagogue that had a small membership, and as a teenager I would often eat dinner late after having been pressed into service as the 10th man for evening prayers.

Dora and Karl's social sense extended beyond helping people. Both were rather gregarious. My father would say: "You talk to everybody. Everybody has different experiences. You can learn from everybody, even the drunk on the corner." Everybody came to our house. The relatives came, the neighbors came. Everyone was welcome. Although we were not well-off, my mother was a great magician. During those visits she was always able to make food and coffee materialize for everyone.

This sociability also extended beyond those with whom we had family or communal ties. Around the block from my father's tailor shop was St. Finbarr's Catholic Church. The priests and members of the church would come to the shop and stand around kibitzing, discussing all sorts of things.

Every year St. Finbarr's would have a carnival, and my father would tell me: "You've got to take a little money and spend it over there – they're our neighbors."

Then there was an African-American man named Mr. Johnson, who lived in the neighborhood and asked to set up a shoeshine booth in a corner of my father's shop. Karl never charged him rent, even though he offered to pay. My father thought: Here's a man who wants to work to earn a few dollars, and the space isn't being used, so let him try.

Jewish social life revolved around the *vereins* and the synagogues, and my father became president of a small congregation. He also became friendly with the precinct captain and the politicians in the area, and he used those contacts to help the members of his synagogue. At one time the neighborhood political bosses offered him a job in the local Democratic Party, but he turned them down.

"I don't want anything for myself," he told them, "but I want you to take care of the people in my synagogue" – whatever they needed, whether it was food during the holidays or more garbage cans. This is how I learned that if you're in government, you're in government to help people.

It was a different world, not only in terms of work ethic but also community ties. People spent time together. There was no air conditioning, so on hot days people would sit outside on the stoops or on benches and talk together, argue with each other, listen to one another.

Despite the hard economic times, we moved forward with a positive outlook. In school I always had friends even though I wasn't athletic or popular. And I knew that I came from a family where I was wanted and loved by my parents. They had their disagreements and arguments, but I always had the feeling that no matter what, things were going to turn out all right.

On my last birthday I turned 81. Through the years I have come to the conclusion that what you want to do, you will do well. What you don't want to do, you will not do well. And you have to have some fire in your belly to do what you want to do.

I learned about that fire from my high school friend Davey Kaplan. I was not a great student, but Davey was without doubt the smartest kid in our class and maybe all of Marshall High School. He told me to stop goofing off, settle down and take learning seriously, because learning can be fun. The more you learn, the more the world opens up around you and with it, opportunity. This thinking turned my life around. Davey went on to become a professor and nuclear physicist, but he died of Parkinson's at a relatively young age. His influence helped push me in the right direction and onto many right paths.

And on those paths I have been very fortunate. I am grateful for all that I have had and all that I have been able to achieve in my 42-year career in public service. I got married at 21 while I was still in law school. My wife, Charlotte, worked to support us then, and we lived for a while with my parents and then her parents. We had three children who have become good people in their own right, and they have given us six wonderful grandchildren.

I have been able to do the things that I wanted to do. When I was young I wanted to make sure that I wasn't a Democrat just because my father was a Democrat. I went to Republican Party events and to Socialist Party events to distill my own political philosophy. I came to the conclusion early on that few people believe in any one philosophy 100 percent, but the Democratic Party stood for much of what I believed.

I became a lawyer and taught law. I ran for office and was elected to the Illinois House of Representatives for seven terms, representing suburban districts of Cook County north of Chicago. Then I became a Cook County Circuit Court judge for 20 years. A few months after retiring from the bench, I was appointed chairman of the Illinois Gaming Board, which regulates casino and video gaming.

I was serving in the Illinois legislature in 1972, the year President Nixon was re-elected. A group of left-wing activists in my district invited local politicians from across the spectrum to analyze the election results. The Republican on the panel got up and talked about how fortunate it was for the country that Nixon would serve a second term, and the audience was steaming. Representing the Democrats, I got up and said that my party had lost the election. I outlined what we stood for and what we should have done. There was little I could add to the discussion.

Then the Socialist Party representative got up and said: "I don't want to talk about elections. We don't need an election – we need a revolution. We need bullets, not ballots." I was listening to him, and I smiled.

Then the guy from the Communist Party got up and said: "We need a revolution, but the problem with him [the guy from the Socialist Party] is that he doesn't know how to stage a revolution. *We* know how to stage a revolution." I was listening with a big smile on my face.

Then a man in the audience stood up and said: "Hey, Jaffe, is it ballots or bullets, is it election or revolution?" And I said: "I do think we need a revolution. But I'm working in the state legislature. I'm trying to get better education for children. I want to make sure kids have a good breakfast before they go to school every day. And because I'm working to bring about reform, I can't really get involved in your revolution. So the two of you should figure out how you're going to make that revolution. Until then, I'm going to be in the legislature."

I knew that if you're going to change things, you can't do it just by sitting on the outside and telling everyone what is wrong, just by crying and blowing your nose. You have to get on the inside and do the insider fighting if you're going to change things. And that's not easy.

By engaging in the give-and-take in the legislature and the balancing act in the courtroom, and having parried as a regulator with governors and legislators, I have been able to do what I have wanted to do – which is to try to bring about positive change from within.

On this path I feel as if I have had an angel on my shoulder looking out for me. That angel represents the amalgam of family, friends, colleagues and community to which I am connected, an amalgam that is something bigger, something greater than myself.

In all this, I think I have lived my own American dream.

And I think that everyone should have the chance, in his or her own life, to have the same kind of opportunities that I have had, and to live his or her own American dream.

The great territorial and economic expansion of the United States in the decades leading up to the Depression occurred with relatively little government involvement in people's lives. Some people put their money in banks, but the banks were neither insured nor regulated. When people lost their jobs, there was no unemployment compensation. Society was not regulated to protect people; it was controlled for the sake of moneyed interests, in particular the great industrialists of the day and the banks that capitalized them.

Because the government provided no fallback provisions for the people, they suffered in massive proportions when the economy collapsed. During the Depression many, including the upper middle class, saw their life savings go down the drain.

So it was necessary for the government to step in and do the things that Franklin Delano Roosevelt did under the New Deal. It was often said then that capitalism was dying, and there was great fear in the United States that the country would turn fascist. So FDR used a little bit of socialism to pump life into the capitalist system – and it began to work.

It became obvious from the circumstances of the Depression that in order to have a healthy society, the government had to intervene to protect the people's basic interests. This was not a new concept.

In biblical times Joseph was in Egypt during a famine. When the pharaoh summoned him for advice, Joseph told the king to build up reserves during the good years so that the people would have food during the lean years.

That may have been the first government-assistance program. The government gets involved when necessary and balances the economy so that the system works. This protects the people so they can prosper.

The Depression was a wake-up call that certain aspects of the American economy needed to be regulated. In order to save the banks and provide safeguards for people's money, the government stepped in to insure the banks and depositors' accounts. Now the banks had to handle depositors' money prudently, and if banks were going to invest that money, those investments had to be low-risk.

The government didn't insure the investment banks, so if people wanted their money to be safe, they put it in savings banks that were insured. As the government took on the role of regulating the financial system, the people were able to build their savings to a greater degree than ever before, and those savings were now largely protected.

The New Deal social safety net had other strands, including laws providing for Social Security, regulating a minimum wage and outlawing most forms of child labor. In 1944 the GI Bill made higher education available to more Americans than ever before. With our victory in World War II and the economic stimulus it provided, the United States emerged as the No. 1 world power.

Because we were free and our means to advancement were expanding, the country was regenerated. Social programs recharged the American spirit; the rejuvenated economy enabled the development of new industries. We were motivated to prosper. We became the richest and most educated country in the world.

Government didn't become all-powerful, though. It was basically an umpire that called balls and strikes: This is permitted, that isn't allowed. It regulated the financial system to prevent crashes. And this worked as long as the government worked to protect the people's prosperity.

Beginning in the 1980s, though, moneyed interests began to push for change based on the idea that the government had become too large and intrusive in people's lives. Regulation was bad, they argued, and the government should pull back and let the financial markets control themselves and everything else. Today the roster of moneyed interests is reflected in the Washington lobby corps, which is led by the health care, financial, insurance and real estate industries.[2]

Over time the financial markets controlled things not only by themselves but *for* themselves. The Reagan years were the watershed of this thinking; the systematic deregulation of the financial system that took place over the decades that followed opened the floodgates for disaster.

A great political divide in this country has developed between those who support regulation and those who don't, and the arguments often fall along party lines. Democrats have tended to want more regulation; Republicans, less. And from this has emerged perhaps the greatest American political contest of all time: an ongoing fight over what should be regulated, and to what degree.

We have gone beyond the tipping point to where enough of our leaders in the White House and Congress – Republicans and Democrats alike – have agreed over time to let moneyed interests in this country charge whatever interest rates they want; to remove safeguards so financial institutions no longer had to be accountable for how secure their investments were; and to virtually erase the distinction between investment banks and savings banks.

Our government's support for the empowerment of capital has been linked to the expansion of American militarism. Just as the United States was assuming superpower status on the world stage, however, Dwight Eisenhower – a great American general, war hero and president – warned us that while we could not have peace at any price, we were to heed the great costs of war.

Eisenhower had the kind of vision that is sorely lacking among our leaders today, and the words of his 1953 "Cross of Iron" speech still resonate six decades and two generations later:

Every gun that is made, every warship launched, every rocket fired signifies, in the final sense, a theft from those who hunger and are not fed, those who are cold and are not clothed.

This world in arms is not spending money alone. It is spending the sweat of its laborers, the genius of its scientists, the hopes of its children. The cost of one modern heavy bomber is this: a modern brick school in more than 30 cities.

It is two electric power plants, each serving a town of 60,000 population. It is two fine, fully equipped hospitals. ... We pay for a single fighter with a half million bushels of wheat. We pay for a single destroyer with new homes that could have housed more than 8,000 people. ... This is not a way of life at all, in any true sense. Under the cloud of threatening war, it is humanity hanging from a cross of iron. These plain and cruel truths define the peril and point the hope that come with this spring of 1953.[3]

Since World War II, however, we have constantly been at war, with short pauses here and there. The Department of Defense reported that there were 611 U.S. military bases in 39 countries overseas in 2010, just under two-thirds of them in Germany, Japan and South Korea[4] – and not including U.S. bases in Iraq and Afghanistan.

At $698.1 billion, U.S. defense spending for 2010 was more than 2.25 times that of the 27 countries of the European Union, whose spending totaled $299.7 billion. The U.S. committed 4.5 percent of its GDP to military expenditures, nearly triple the EU's 1.63 percent,[5] although its population is almost 60 percent larger than ours.

In 2010 U.S. military spending accounted for about 43 percent – or nearly half – of global military expenditures.[6] We outspend China, which has the second-largest military budget in the world and a population four times the size of ours, by nearly 6 to 1.[7]

At the same time, while the American role in the global capital system has grown, the consequences of a deregulated financial system at home and the imposition of American militarism abroad have come home to roost on all of our heads.

The government is no longer the referee of moneyed interests, including the military-industrial complex, but rather has become their partner. That's one of the main reasons we're facing the troubles we're facing today.

Over the past 30 years, these policies have had the effect of widening the gap in American income levels precipitously, bringing us back to conditions akin to those that prevailed on the eve of the Great Depression. We are going backward when we should be going forward.

In 1928, the year before the Depression began, the top 1 percent of Americans held 24 percent of U.S. income share. However, in the decades following the New Deal, from the early 1950s through the 1980s, the top 1 percentile's income share dropped to between 8 percent and 11 percent – evidence that a growing number of Americans were gaining a greater share of opportunity. But by the time the Great Recession hit at the end of 2007, the top percentile's income share had rocketed back up to about 23.5 percent.[8]

At the other end of the spectrum, developments on the poverty front have been equally grave. In September 2011 the U.S. Census Bureau reported that the nation's official poverty rate in 2010 was 15.1 percent, up from 14.3 percent in 2009. The 46.2 million Americans living in poverty in 2010 represented the fourth consecutive annual increase – and the largest number in the 52 years that poverty estimates have been published.[9]

To make matters worse, political dialogue in this country has ground to a screeching halt and has been replaced by shout fests in which the terms "liberal" and "conservative" are thrown around like sharp-pointed spears. But "liberal" is just a label, and "conservative" is just a label, and we need to get away from labels. Labeling confuses the issues by reducing them to the irreducible.

There is no such thing as a pure "ism"; nothing is absolute. We have to face our problems and ask: What are the best solutions for most of the people? Often the best solutions require a nuanced if not somewhat complex balancing of "isms."

There are two things to be considered when decisions are made in public life: policy and politics. In our society today, most of these decisions are political due to the degree of influence that moneyed interests have gained over our system of government. The two-party system no longer answers to the people but rather to moneyed interests.

Recently we have seen Congress pass health care and financial reform bills that are thousands of pages long. There is no need to have bills that long to state policy and programs, and nobody understands what's in all of those thousands of pages except the lobbyists who wrote them. Laws should be written in language that is understandable to everyone. But this has become increasingly difficult as moneyed interests have come between the people and their government to an unprecedented degree.

So now I drop the other shoe, for my purpose here is not to wax nostalgic about the good old days or to sing a swan song of self-satisfaction. Rather, it is to express my concerns about the course that our country has taken and to do so in the context of how I have come to my ideas through the values I learned early in life and in more than 40 years as a legislator, judge and regulator.

My experience in public life has taken place on somewhat of a local stage, in and around Chicago and in the Illinois state capital. However, the vignettes upon which my observations and conclusions are based transcend the boundaries of locale and the genre of memoir.

The ideas in these pages can resonate for Americans whether they live in suburban Chicago or in the Rocky Mountains or on the Gulf Coast of Florida. Through the prism of my experience, I speak to the roots of our shared national predicament and our common American *zeitgeist*. Thus I hope what follows not only will spur a conversation but also will encourage action that reaches across regions and generations and even classes.

Like many Americans, I am very concerned about the future of our great country. I find the current state of affairs to be something of a disturbing bookend: My life began during the Depression, and now my grandchildren are growing up in a climate that is in some ways similar.

To be sure, they are not now as directly affected by these troubles as I was growing up. But the simple truth of the matter is that it's going to be tougher for my grandchildren to do what they want to do in life than it was for me. The American dream will not likely be as accessible to them as it was to me.

This is a troubling inversion of my father's metaphor of each succeeding generation rising to build a higher floor of the house. Unless we re-establish the paths to opportunity, the coming generations will have a harder and harder time just keeping their footing on the same floor.

We often refer to the American dream as the result of obtaining material goods and a higher standard of living. We often measure the American dream in terms of our ability to consume more. There is tremendous pressure to achieve creature comforts. The culture of consumerism enmeshes us and permeates nearly every facet of our lives.

Our society is chock-full of messages coming at us from every direction imploring us to consume. We turn on the TV and see a constant stream of commercials that tells us what medicines we should take, what soap we should buy, what food we should eat. Advertising permeates the Internet and reaches us even on our cellphones.

If you're rich, the ads seem to imply, things are grand; if you're poor, you're out of luck. Not even subliminally do these messages tell us to judge ourselves on the content of our character, as Dr. Martin Luther King Jr. had dreamed. Rather, these messages tell us to judge ourselves and others on the quality of the stuff that we have acquired.

When we say "America is No. 1," what do we mean? I would hope we mean that we are the best-educated people on the planet and that we are in a position to provide moral leadership to the world. But that's not what we mean. Many Americans think that we're No. 1 because as a country we have the most powerful military machine in the world and as individuals we have the most goodies.

But the American dream is as much about the process of self-actualization as it is about getting the goodies. It's about realizing our potential to the fullest possible extent while encountering the fewest possible barriers.

This raises the pivotal issue of how much of a role government should play in the American dream and how much the individual can and should determine. This question is at the heart of many political issues, even ones that don't refer to the American dream explicitly but are nonetheless infused with its ethos.

I still believe that despite the metamorphosis of our political system in recent decades, American government should be by and for the people. As such, government should not be an alien and intrusive mechanism that stands in the way of people realizing their dreams.

Government certainly cannot and should not provide for all of our needs, and we cannot and should not rely on government to replace the values that ensure individual success: honesty, hard work, responsibility, consistency and the ability to dream beyond what exists today to what we can make possible tomorrow.

When it functions effectively and on a reasonable scale, however, government can and should be the partner of the people in achieving their defense, their security and their fair shot at opportunity. It is only when moneyed interests intervene to the alarming extent that they have over the last 30 years that government is no longer this partner.

I have lived my own American dream by achieving a career in public service – the result of my hard work and that of my family, along with their guidance and moral support. At the same time, government has protected my freedoms of thought and expression and until recently the ability of my family to save and invest the fruits of our labors safely. I also had the benefit of good public schools and affordable higher education.

However, the greatest driver of the American dream has not been government-enabled opportunity. It has been the ability of Americans to see themselves as individuals who have both the grit and the gumption to move forward. But today individualism – the very thing that made this country great – is on the wane.

This has resulted from an explosion of largeness in the marketplace. Government has become the advocate of corporations and rich individuals at the expense of ordinary Americans, whose opportunities to self-actualize are increasingly constricted. This has led to feelings of malaise and powerlessness to which we cannot succumb.

I too am finding it harder to maintain my own happy warrior mindset – the feeling that no matter what happens, things will be fine. Now something tells me that things may not be fine. Unless we take corrective action, we may go the way of other great civilizations and face our own decline.

We have to be honest with ourselves, and in this country we are not honest with one another. It is becoming more and more difficult to find truthfulness emanating from the government, from the mainstream media – from many of the very institutions that we once relied on and respected. This lack of respect and truthfulness is absolutely disastrous.

We are going to have to re-examine our society from top to bottom. While it's human nature to point the finger and to blame others, we're going to have to look in the mirror and not only take responsibility for ourselves as individuals but also make sure that our society is governed properly and that our institutions are run right.

To get back on track, we need to have a national conversation. Here are some starting points for discussion:

Why are our politics no longer of the people?

Why do our leaders substitute political expediency for public policy so often by taking the easy way out?

Why is our political culture suffering from such a profound listening deficit?

And if we don't take action, are we going to lose our American dream?

2
A Politics Not of the People

When I was growing up, we had a politics that revolved around the people. The country was in big trouble. People did not have enough to eat, people were not being educated, people were downtrodden. The questions floating around my neighborhood were: How are we going to elevate our society? How can people earn a good living and advance? That's what politics was all about.

Two generations later, we are facing many of the same questions but in a different framework. For decades American society hummed along according to the axiomatic notions that we have a superior form of government. That no other country does it better than we do. That everything will always be OK – even when times get hard, we'll get through because we are a wonderful people who have the right stuff and who do the right thing.

This thinking went hand in glove with the pronouncements of those in the top echelons of government, right down to (or up to) the head of the Federal Reserve. For two decades as Fed chairman, Alan Greenspan told Americans: Just let this marvelous free market go unregulated, and it will take you to heaven. And we believed it.

Beginning in the 1980s, we were also increasingly told that the regulation of the financial markets that had brought more of us prosperity had become unnecessary because Wall Street and the free market were infallible, almost religiously so. But when we reached the brink of collapse in 2008, what did Greenspan (by then out of office) say? He said: Whoops, I think I miscalculated.

What did the free-market advocates embedded deeply within the highest ranks of our government prescribe to prevent our battered economy from grinding to a complete halt? The free-marketeers said: Let's feed the big banks and investment houses, let's bail them out because they are too big to fail, and everything will be OK. So we, the taxpayers, bailed them out. And we also bailed out AIG, the insurance company that insured the big banks.

But what is the result? We see that the big banks and the investment houses on Wall Street are doing well, some much better than ever before. But what's happening to us, the people?

We have a real estate market that has collapsed, reeling from monumental numbers of foreclosures. We have a high unemployment rate that has been more or less constant for four years.

We have young Americans who have graduated from college and can't find jobs that pay living wages. At the same time, they have accumulated educational debt that will take years, if not decades, to pay off. But these young people cannot discharge their debt in bankruptcy, because the banks that lent them money had lobbyists make certain that the laws would be written so as not to allow these loans to be discharged in bankruptcy.

So is it any wonder that the people who are being squeezed so tightly by the economy and who at the same time are watching the rich get richer got angry? That they got angry because they see that their government is doing little to help them – but it continues, through its policies, to take the side of the wealthy?

That anger spurred the Occupy Wall Street movement. Beginning in September 2011, protestors began to spill into the streets across the country, their anger breaking the dams of frustration over the status quo. They marched by the thousands – at the Port of Oakland, outside the doors of City Hall in Chicago, on the Brooklyn Bridge.

The Occupy protesters have taken to the streets because corporate Wall Street is bloodless and soulless: It cares little about the average American and worships its own bottom line. At the same time, our political system has evolved into one that encourages if not requires many of our elected officials to occupy themselves with how they will raise the money to get re-elected, in significant measure from corporate interests that are represented on Wall Street.

So average Americans have started to feel helpless, and fueled by their pent-up anger, they have begun to protest. But being Americans, our demonstrations are peaceful, because we expect our pleas to be heard and heeded by the people whom we elected to represent our interests.

In the first couple of weeks that the Occupy movement materialized, the mainstream media, which report diligently on what Lindsay Lohan is wearing every time she appears in court, gave sparse coverage to the unfolding protests.

Then one day the protestors blocked traffic on the Brooklyn Bridge, and the media were compelled to note their existence. But what did the media report? They told us that the protestors are misguided and lack focus, that they are a bunch of would-be hippies. Wait 'til winter, the pundits opined, and it will be too cold for them to protest. The mainstream media fixated on the circuses to the near exclusion of the bread, which is the issues that brought the protestors into the streets in the first place.

Meanwhile, advocates for the interests of big capital, both inside and outside of our government, have described the protests using epithets including "class warfare" and "un-American" – as if the protestors were breaching some sort of social compact or committing some kind of crime.

But the Occupy movement has within its ranks people who represent America's future. These people are not the enemy. These people are waking America up.

All the while, what have the people in government been talking about? They say we must create new jobs, but they can't even agree among themselves to pass the $450 billion job-creation bill. Instead, some among them advocate slashing public-sector programs, even though this will have the opposite effect: Not only will these cuts deny Americans some vital programs and services, but the cuts will also take away the jobs of the people who provide them.

By early November 2011, less than two months after the Occupy protest movement began, a Pew Research Center analysis of U.S. Census data revealed a stunning trend – evidence that the young Occupy protestors are not misguided in the least. The study reported that the wealth gap between younger and older Americans has reached historic proportions: In 2009 the typical U.S. household headed by a person 65 or older had a net worth 47 times greater than a household headed by someone under 35.[1]

Acknowledging that people typically accumulate assets as they age, the Pew analysis noted that this generational wealth gap "is now more than double what it was in 2005 and nearly five times the 10-to-1 disparity a quarter-century ago [1984], after adjusting for inflation." The primary reasons for the dramatic widening of the wealth gap: housing debt, educational debt and unemployment.[2]

The only way that we're going to be able to begin to reverse this trend and start to turn the economy around is not by feeding the rich but by investing public funds to increase opportunities for everyone from the bottom up. The government bailouts of the last few years have made it perfectly clear that corporate welfare does not translate to job creation, and that trickle-down theories of spreading prosperity from top to bottom don't pan out.

Critics of the Occupy protestors fail to understand a basic tenet of history, which applies even to Americans: If the majority of the people are suppressed for too long, eventually the people rebel. At this time of great national distress, we have started to turn a corner – and despite attempts to marginalize or even vilify the protestors, there will be no going back. The American people are waking up.

And as more of us wake up, we're not going to join the fat cats or the politicians who serve them. We're going to join the people in the streets. And when we do that, remarkable things are going to happen.

Tired of the road to greed and oligarchy, the people will press harder for a change of course. They will demand a road that takes them back to fair play and democracy, a road that takes them back to equalized opportunity, a road that once again gives them a fair shot at the American dream.

And it will be at their own peril that those in government ignore or seek to marginalize those who are trying to reclaim a politics of the people.

I had the good fortune to come into my political awareness at a time when there were a few great men. During the Depression Roosevelt instituted programs that would change the country dramatically. Then along came Harry S. Truman, a man who had been a farmer, a haberdasher. He had gone broke in business. He was not a college graduate, but he was self-educated. He had read his way through the Independence, Missouri, public library.

Truman became an army captain in World War I, and his troops adored him because he was a good leader. He lacked a commanding physical presence, and the beginning of his political career was nondescript. He took a minor position in state government but did a wonderful job at it, and all of a sudden he started to rise.

Among all the political machinations, here was a very decent guy doing a very decent job. He ran for senator and won, then during World War II he headed a special congressional committee that investigated practices of U.S. military contractors. He uncovered a great deal of mismanagement and corruption but still was not considered a heavy hitter in the Senate. In 1944 Roosevelt tapped Truman as his running mate, thinking: We can sell him to everyone, because no one has anything against him.

As vice president, Truman was the last person FDR confided in; Truman didn't even know that we were working on the atomic bomb. When Roosevelt died, Truman became president, but he still talked like a farmer. But here's what he did: He ended the war, he started the Marshall Plan to rebuild Europe and he strongly supported the creation of the United Nations. His initiatives rehabilitated the United States and the world.

I graduated high school in 1948, a presidential election year. Truman was running, and the press and pollsters reported that he was a terrible candidate. He had image problems and political problems. People didn't like him because he wasn't FDR.

In those days both parties had platforms that they would fight about for days at their conventions. That year Hubert Humphrey, then mayor of Minneapolis, stepped forward and said: We must have a civil-rights plank in the Democratic Party platform. Speaking for southern Democrats, South Carolina Gov. Strom Thurmond told

Truman: If you put that plank in the platform, we're going to leave the party.

Before 1948 the South was called "the solid South" because it voted solidly for the Democratic Party. Truman faced a political decision, but he insisted on keeping the civil-rights plank. The South walked, and there were some southern states in which Truman's name didn't even appear on the ballot, with Thurmond leading the segregationist Dixiecrats instead.

Truman stuck to his principles and paid the political price. He won the election, but after 1948 the South began to move increasingly toward becoming the solidly Republican base that it is today.

Truman was basically an everyman, a guy who came out of nowhere. His record wasn't perfect, but on balance he did a lot of good, especially considering that he was the underdog who couldn't fill FDR's shoes. In October 1948 the pollsters projected that there was no way Truman was going to win the election. He was not popular, and his campaign war chest was meager at best.

He traveled the country making speeches on his famous whistle-stop tour, and on election night the *Chicago Tribune* jumped the gun and printed the infamous headline "Dewey defeats Truman." But Harry S. Truman won, and he became my hero. Not only was he a man of action, but he was also a man of conscience – and a man of the people.

These days men and women of the people are becoming increasingly few and far between in the American political landscape because the barriers to entry have become exceedingly high. In 2010 the average winning U.S. congressional campaign was estimated to cost $1.5 million, requiring incumbents to raise about $15,000 a week.[3]

Total spending on the 2010 federal midterm elections has been estimated at a whopping $4 billion (with at least $293 million of the total spent by interest groups vying to affect the outcomes).[4] By contrast, in the 1986 congressional campaign, candidates across the country spent a total of about $300 million.[5]

The campaign in 2008, a presidential election year, was the costliest on record at $5.3 billion spent by candidates, political parties and interest groups in congressional and presidential races, according to the Washington-based watchdog Center for Responsive Politics. This represented a 27 percent increase over the $4.2 billion spent in the 2004 presidential and congressional campaigns. The amount spent on the 2008 presidential race alone was $2.4 billion, with party nominees Barack Obama and John McCain together spending more than $1 billion.[6]

By contrast, in the 1996 election cycle, the Clinton and Dole campaigns spent about $232 million, supplemented by about $69 million in issue ads paid for by the Republican and Democratic national committees. Across the country, congressional election campaigns in 1996 cost about $2.7 billion.[7] Within four election cycles presidential nominees had more than tripled their spending, with more than half of these expenditures estimated to go to media costs.[8]

The realms of campaign fundraising and lobbying overlap to a significant degree, with lobbyists, by one account, constituting "the most important fundraisers in the money grind, because they serve as lawmakers' links to the most promising donors: those with business interests related to each member's committee assignments."[9]

Case in point: The 43 members of the House-Senate conference committee on financial reform legislation that was passed in 2010 had, since 1989, collectively received $112 million in campaign contributions from donors associated with the finance, insurance and real estate industries.[10]

Meanwhile, in October 2011 *The New York Times* reported that President Obama had relied on at least 15 bundlers – supporters who contribute their own money and solicit it from others – to raise more than $5 million for his re-election campaign. Although not registered lobbyists, these bundlers who helped fill Obama's campaign coffers were, according to the *Times*, "prominent supporters who are active in the lobbying industry." Obama refused contributions from registered federal lobbyists and political action committees; Republican candidates, by contrast, had reportedly placed no restrictions on accepting money from lobbyists.[11]

I ran the campaigns for my seven terms in the Illinois House of Representatives from 1970 to 1984 in a different universe. Of course, these were not national campaigns, and it was an era when big money and big media had not yet altered the political landscape from top to bottom. If I spent $10,000 on a campaign, that was a massive amount of money. Today a state rep candidate needs hundreds of thousands of dollars to run a campaign. If I had to raise money the way politicians do now, I doubt I would have gone into politics.

I was a terrible fundraiser. Asking people for money so I could run for office was just about the worst thing I had to do. In all the years I ran for office, I did it on very little money. When we had fundraisers, they were $10 or $25 a head, and we'd give people a dinner for that.

These fundraisers were fun events to bring people out, to get people to work on the campaign. We had ice cream socials with silent movies. We held fundraisers at bowling alleys, and people bowled. We had fundraisers at bars – "speak out at the speakeasy" – and it was great fun to see my fellow politicians get up, say something silly and get hooked off the stage.

During a campaign in the middle of my legislative career, one of my political friends told me that I needed to hire a professional fundraiser. Everyone is starting to use them, my friend said, and they're good. They can go out and get money for you.

So I met with a fundraiser, and he told me how I would have to go after certain people, talk to them, make calls, and he would give me an entrée. What he described bothered me, though. Not only did I find the idea of going to people for money distasteful, but it also would have changed the way I ran my campaigns. Having to ask for handouts would have meant spending most of my time doing the thing I didn't like to do, and it would have taken me further and further away from the people I was running to represent.

The fundraiser would have sent me to people who would give me money, and when they did that, they would become my new best friends. But some of these new best friends inhabited places I didn't want to go for money. I didn't want to become beholden to such people, and I found the idea of selling myself for money to be repugnant.

My campaigns were people campaigns. We worked the streets and stuck to the issues. In the end I didn't work with the fundraiser. I was responsible for my own campaigns; their tone and tenor were mine and mine alone.

But political campaigns were getting more expensive, and they started to use marketing tactics. Not too long after

I left office, candidates were spending more on one campaign for the legislature than I had spent in 14 years. You had to advertise in the newspapers and in the ad books of civic and charitable organizations. There were mailings and there were trinkets: buttons, bumper stickers, key chains. Political ads on TV were becoming more prevalent.

I resisted the marketing approach as much as I could. I was the type of politician who stood in front of the supermarket, who visited the delis. I would do one mailing and then would reach out to people by going door to door and making public appearances by the dozen. I went to every group that invited me: PTAs, business associations, fraternal organizations. I was all over the place.

Being that accessible was a tough job, but I did it and I enjoyed it. I'd do coffee hours in people's homes and maybe raise a few dollars – but I used those events to solicit volunteers more than funds. Today candidates appear at cocktail parties where guests are expected to drop large sums, anywhere from hundreds to tens of thousands of dollars, depending on the stature of the candidate.

The fact that campaigns were changing and money was becoming more of a driving factor was not lost on me. But I resisted letting that change the way I ran for office.

By 1960 I was practicing law, and Charlotte and I had two children. We did what many upwardly mobile families were doing – we moved to the suburbs, just north of Chicago. I became a precinct captain for my neighborhood in Skokie that year, which was a presidential election year. The precinct captain makes personal contact with the voters in the district on behalf of a political party and/or its candidate. It was an unpaid job, and I did it because I loved politics.

At the time I didn't have much interest in local government, and people asked me why I wanted to get involved in politics in a place where the Democratic township committeeman had a reputation for being gruff and inaccessible. His name was Scotty Krier, and I would have to go through him if I wanted in.

So I called Scotty and got him on the phone right away. "I want to come to see you about working the election," I said. He asked me: "What are you doing now?" I said: "I'm talking to you on the phone." That same afternoon I met with Scotty in his office, and he appointed me a precinct captain.

He turned out not to be the difficult character that he was said to be. Like my father said: You talk to everyone and you learn the truth for yourself. By talking to Scotty, I found that he was more liberal than most people in the community. But somehow he had gotten a bad rap.

Illinois has a storied history of political corruption, not the least of which has played out in Chicago and the rest of

Cook County. What's not widely known or understood, though, is that at one time the county's underlying political structure went a long way toward keeping the people strongly connected to their politics.

Cook County is divided into 30 townships; the city of Chicago has 50 wards. Wards and townships are divided into precincts, and each precinct has approximately 500 voters. Each ward and township elects a Republican committeeman and a Democratic committeeman, and they are responsible for running each party's organization in that area.

Committeemen recruited the precinct captains, who got the party's message out by knocking on doors, talking to people, hearing people's opinions and letting people know what the party stood for. Precinct captains also made sure that people knew about the parties' candidates, and on Election Day the captains got out the vote.

I was among the last of the old-time precinct captains. When I worked a precinct, or later my district as a candidate for the state legislature, I would go out every week night and weekend door to door. That's how it was done when I first got into the legislature, and I was one of the last to campaign that way.

It was not an easy job. I rang the doorbells of about 250 households, and I had to psych myself up to do it. But most people welcomed me into their homes. Only one person slammed the door in my face. I was working the precinct, and I came to a house and rang the bell. There was no answer, so I rang it again and then a third time.

Finally a man opened the door. He looked bedraggled, like he had just gotten out of bed. I said: "Hello, I'm Aaron Jaffe, and I'm your Democratic precinct captain." And he slammed the door in my face. I thought maybe he was going through a hard time, so I waited two weeks and then went back. When he opened the door, I said: "Hello, remember me?" And he slammed the door in my face again.

By and large, though, people wanted to talk, and they wanted to know. So I went to every house and talked to people. I would even ring the doorbell of the Republican precinct captain's house and talk to him and his wife for a while. I might have even gotten her vote.

It was hard to get people to work a precinct. It had been easier in bad economic times because of the patronage system. The party rewarded many people who worked the elections with jobs in government. Over time, though, the public began to view precinct captains as hacks who did the bidding of political parties, who did favors and were not good for the political system. There was more to it than that, though.

There were hacks. But precinct captains went out and talked to people in the community about the party and its candidates. And if precinct captains were good at what they did, they would find out what people were thinking, and they would come back and report to the committeeman. Because the party wanted your vote, you could be sure that if people felt a certain way, the party would fall in line.

Over time the patronage system was no more. It was needed less as a source of jobs as people got more affluent, especially in the suburbs. The public came to dislike the patronage system because they associated it with ward bosses and corruption. But today there's more corruption than ever before. In those days it was nickel-and-dime stuff; now it's in the millions.

There was a time in Cook County when if you asked people who their precinct captain was, 80 or 90 percent could tell you. Today people will ask you what a precinct captain is or say they haven't seen one in 20 years. Nowadays precinct captains mostly walk around and drop literature. They don't talk to people much anymore, because people have a different mindset about political parties.

When I became Niles Township Democratic committeeman in 1969, I put together an organization that was about 25 percent old-time precinct captains and 75 percent volunteers, new people who were politically motivated and dedicated to issues and philosophy.

We started to do things that were a little unusual for a political organization. The first public meeting that I held as committeeman was about the Vietnam War. I invited a poet and a speaker who were not mainstream. The tone of the meeting was somewhat anti-war – even though the national Democratic Party supported the war.

My predecessor as committeeman, Ray Krier (Scotty's son), said to me: "Are you nuts? Why are you holding this type of meeting? You're going to destroy the organization."

"Ray," I said, "don't worry about it. This is what people in our township are thinking." I knew that because we had our people out on the street, working the neighborhoods and talking to people. We held the meeting, and we didn't lose workers or the people's support. As a matter of fact, more people joined our organization.

As township committeeman I organized public debates on a range of issues. We invited people from the Daley machine in Chicago to debate. We had a group of young people who went to Iowa to stack sandbags when there were floods. Ours wasn't the ordinary Democratic Party organization. We did things.

I ran my own political campaigns for the state legislature along the same lines. My campaigns were primarily people campaigns. We put people on the street, and they weren't there just to drop literature – they were there to talk to voters.

I was constantly on the street when I ran for office. If you walked into the supermarket, in all probability I was there shopping and talking to people. If you walked into the restaurants or delis, I would be there. I lived in the neighborhood, so I was accessible.

My nephew lives in a northwest suburb. His next-door neighbor had once lived in my district. My nephew asked him, "Do you know my uncle?" The neighbor started to laugh and said: "Do I know your uncle? I know your uncle. Your uncle is crazy."

My nephew started to take offense: "If you thought my uncle was crazy, then you probably never voted for him."

Neighbor: "Not only did I vote for him, I used to work for him in the precinct."

Nephew: "So if you thought he was crazy, why did you vote for him?"

Neighbor: "Because I could call him on the phone, I could talk to him anytime I wanted, I could argue with him – and I knew that he listened. And I never had anyone in politics listen to me before."

That kind of connection made all the difference in my most difficult campaign. It was 1972, my first re-election bid for the state legislature. At the time I was still also the Niles Township Democratic committeeman. My legislative district covered only 25 percent of Niles Township; the majority of the district was in Maine Township.

Nick Blase was mayor of the village of Niles, and he was also the Maine Township Democratic committeeman. He controlled most of the area that was in my legislative district. Nick called me and said, "Aaron, I'm going to run for Congress against Abner Mikva."

Mikva, who would later become a federal judge and counsel to President Clinton, was also running on the Democratic ticket for Congress at that time in the district that encompassed Maine and Niles townships. Nick was a conservative Democrat; Ab was more liberal.

Nick didn't ask me, he told me: "Aaron, as Niles Township Democratic committeeman, you're going to endorse me for Congress." I told him: "You and I have completely different political views, and Ab and I have pretty similar political views. If I endorse you, that would be contrary to what I stand for. I'd lose my credibility in the political world."

Nick repeated that he was the Maine Township committeeman and that he controlled most of my legislative district. And so it went:

"Well, Nick," I said, "I understand that."

"So you're going to endorse me," he said.

"Nick, you're just not getting it. You and I are just not on the same page politically."

"If you don't endorse me," he said, "you're not going to carry my area."

"I'm sorry," I told him, "but I'm not going to endorse you, and that's it."

And I didn't endorse him. So he ran another Democrat against me, a former state rep who had been very popular and had run in parts of the district where I had not run before. Two Democrats and two Republicans were running for three seats in this predominantly Republican area, so only one Democrat would win.

The candidate Nick ran against me was the heavy favorite; when he got in the race, I was pegged as the loser. Fortunately, though, I had the better organization, because the people working Mikva's campaign also worked for me.

The organization was a people organization; we had people on the street all over the place. We took on Nick's Maine Township Democratic organization, which had prepared a victory party for my opponent. It was like "Dewey defeats Truman" all over again.

But I won a rather substantial victory because I carried Maine Township. We had campaign workers who visited every house in the area and covered it much more thoroughly than Nick's organization had. There was a large unincorporated area in Maine Township that Nick didn't work the way he should have, and we beat him there and in Niles Township.

For the next three elections it was a grudge match: Nick always ran a candidate against me. After a while he understood that his candidates weren't going to win, but he was out to do me as much damage as he possibly could. By the late '70s, when I was carrying every precinct in Maine Township, Nick called me and said: "We ought to bury the hatchet." And I said: "Good idea." So we buried the hatchet, and he supported me from then on.

The power of precinct organization was the power of staying connected to the people. We won because we could organize on the street level. I always maintained that if I could get 100 people to work an area of 60,000 for six weeks, I could win. They would give me their week nights and weekends and go out and work the precincts.

But today candidates can't get 100 in 60,000 to work an area that way – because by and large, the people have lost the connection to their politics.

Today I doubt that you can have a political organization like I did or run campaigns the way I ran them. Things started to change because the political organizations started to die. They died because they couldn't engage the people anymore. Today many people just don't want to get involved. They would rather talk about how terrible things are than do something about it.

Doing something about it was the old politics, but until very recently, there were few signs of people being stirred to take collective action across America. As Americans became more affluent, we began to take more things for granted. Now we're in an era when many people are not so affluent as they used to be, and we can no longer afford to do little but grumble.

When Americans forget that they *are* the government, this doesn't help preserve the American dream. Perhaps the Occupy movement will gain the power it will take to jog our collective memory about the way our government is supposed to work and to spur even more people to action.

The change in how political parties and candidates connect with the people is one reason for people becoming distanced from their politics. The infusion of big money is another. Changes in media coverage of politics have also served to magnify the disconnect.

Television was not a major factor when I started to become politically aware just after high school. TV didn't become significant in politics until 1960, when John F. Kennedy and Richard Nixon held the first televised presidential debates. They held their first debate in Chicago on Sept. 26, and people who watched it on TV thought that JFK had scored a runaway win.

Kennedy was this handsome, young guy debating Nixon, who had a 5 o'clock shadow and looked nervous. But in press coverage of the debate, and to many people who had listened to it on the radio, Nixon had actually sounded more in command.

On the night of the first debate, Democratic political organizations in the northern suburbs of Chicago held a dinner for JFK. The debate had really charged everyone up, because most of us had watched it on TV. When JFK walked down the center aisle of the banquet hall, many of us – women and men alike – were taken aback by his movie-star good looks.

That was the beginning of politics starting to change because of the impact that television had on people's perceptions. But TV coverage was not available to people who were running for offices other than the presidency because it cost too much.

As the patronage system got weaker, the connection between voters and party leaders got looser, and the media steadily became more influential in the political process. Journalists were writing about how good things were and how bad things were, and people believed what they read. There was a respectable print media, with giants such as Walter Lippmann, and on TV the likes of Edward R. Murrow – intellectuals who really understood the system.

Today most people get their news from television, but many TV news shows feature a bunch of talking heads who emphasize partisanship and do so at high-decibel levels. Much TV news has become more entertainment than reporting. The 24/7 networks have to fill time, and it's expensive to keep reporters out in the field. Reporting news based on fact has been supplanted by producing news as a mélange of competing opinions.

This has been a slow shift, but today the 24/7 news cycle on TV and on the Internet produces a constant bombardment of chatter, shifting political discourse away from the issues and toward personality contests. A lot of what comes over the airwaves and through the ether is junk, with political actors cultivating celebrity status by turning their names into brands like Blago and Palin.

More than that, many who convey the information, like Glenn Beck and Rush Limbaugh, strive to become celebrities themselves. The ones on the left scream at the ones on the right, and the ones on the right scream at the ones on the left. It has become a battle of personalities, such as Olbermann vs. Hannity, but they're not the issue.

The issues are getting drowned out in the shout fests, and even those media outlets that don't stoop to tabloid entertainment are influenced by those that do, and the result is less and less substance most of the way around.

Media coverage of national political conventions is a case in point. The conventions used to function not only to nominate the parties' presidential candidates but also to establish policy platforms. Now the policies of the parties are formulated in back rooms with few people looking on, and party platforms, when they exist, have become so vague that they don't mean much anymore.

I was a delegate to the Democratic National Convention in 1972, which nominated George McGovern in Miami

Beach. We engaged in many policy fights, among them how to broaden the party's base to include more women and minorities and, of course, debates over the Vietnam War.

When McGovern was nominated, he was supposed to deliver his acceptance speech in a national primetime TV broadcast. But the policy fights went on for so long that when he finally did speak, it was in the middle of the night, and only a small portion of the American public heard him.

Since then, conventions have been streamlined for TV, and the networks don't televise floor fights anymore. The networks used to broadcast what was happening on the floor all day long, but now convention coverage is packaged for easy listening, an hour or two each night.

This is based on the assumption that people don't want to know how the sausage is being made – but don't they? It may be a bit distasteful, but at one time we actually got to see people struggling over the issues. We don't get to see that struggle anymore, and that distances us further from the sense that we are participating in shaping the future of our country.

Even when I was campaigning, though, a lot of people were not motivated to vote and would say they didn't have time to vote. I had to drag them to the polls, drive them, find babysitters for their kids – anything that would get them out on Election Day. That diminished impetus to get out and vote came with increasing affluence.

Over time advances in communications technology were added to the mix. Today people don't have the same desire to go out and work for candidates or to push for political ideals because so much comes at them through TV and the Internet. It's easier to get the information, but with that ease comes an even greater degree of passivity.

The stakes in the money game have risen dramatically since I was a state legislator in the 1970s and '80s. But the game was played then, too, and special interests tried to have their way with legislators. Back then the proportions were different, though, and the money game was somewhat less of a driving force, both in terms of how you got into office and how you tried to do the people's business once you were there.

Keeping away from the money game and maintaining a loose-cannon status was my modus operandi. I worked for legislation that advanced the public good and opposed legislation that didn't, regardless of what interest groups were lined up on either side of a given issue. That was my method, and sometimes it worked, other times it didn't.

When I first was elected to the Illinois House of Representatives in 1970, I thought I would go down to Springfield and come up with terrific programs that would benefit humanity. I thought I could contribute to curing some of the ills of society.

In my first term, some patients'-rights groups brought to my attention the fact that seniors were being mistreated in certain psychiatric hospitals and other public and private health facilities. These groups asked me to submit a bill to protect seniors from such abuse – a kind of patients' bill of rights.

It was one of the first bills I sponsored. It passed the House and then came to the Senate. I appeared before the Senate committee, and the first question the chairman asked me was: "Who wants this bill?"

I said: "Senator, I don't quite understand what you mean by that. This bill is needed because certain patients'-rights groups have told me that seniors are being abused in various institutions and they need to be protected."

The chairman responded: "Come on, let's not play around. Who wants this bill? Do you want to get somebody out of the nuthouse?" And I said, "Senator, I have no one that I want to get out of the nuthouse, but after appearing before this committee, I can think of some who I would like to put in."

Suffice it to say that my bill was defeated because the chairman thought that bills came from interest groups, and he couldn't grasp what interest group was behind this one. He couldn't comprehend the idea that a bill could just be good legislation to benefit the people. He thought that we were there to serve the interests of various and sundry groups, and he wanted to know what the politics behind the bill were, who the money people were. And in this case there were none, because in those days there were few nonprofit advocacy groups pushing legislation.

At the beginning of every legislative session, the party leaders make committee assignments. At the start of one session, I got my committee assignments and found myself on the banking committee. I thought that was curious, because I knew people who loved being on the banking committee, but I was not one of them. It didn't interest me because my thrust was social policy, especially education.

So I went to see the speaker of the House, Michael Madigan, and I asked him: "Mike, why did you put me on the banking committee? There are plenty of people who want to be on it."

Madigan laughed and said: "I have to put an odd number of people on this committee, and here's my problem. There is a fight between the big banks and the small banks over branch banking. So I assigned an even number of people to the committee who support the small banks' position, and I assigned an even number of people who support the big banks. I looked around, and I found that you didn't support either side. So that's why I assigned you to the banking committee. Have fun."

I sat on that committee with the six who supported the big banks and the six who supported the small banks. The small banks didn't want branch banking because they believed that it would put a lot of them out of business. The big banks prevailed nationwide, and to this day they get preferential regulatory treatment.

At the time I served on the banking committee in the Illinois House, there were lobbyists, but not to the extent that there are today. The legislators who were friendly to the big banks voted the way the big banks wanted them to vote. They were influenced by market philosophy or campaign contributions or both. The same was true for those who supported the small banks.

I sat on the committee watching the trains go by. I tried to figure out what was good for the consumer, but you don't get far when yours is the only vote for consumers in a fight dominated by interest groups.

Fights between interest groups play out often in the legislature. Illinois has two strong teachers unions, the Illinois Federation of Teachers and the Illinois Education Association. In my second term I picked up a bill that my friend Tony Scariano, a Democrat from the south suburbs of Chicago and one of the founders of the liberal Democratic group in the House, had pushed but had not been able to pass before he left the legislature.

Tony's bill would have provided teachers with independent hearing officers in the event that a teacher was facing dismissal. If the superintendent of a school district wanted to fire a teacher, the superintendent would go to the school board. If the school board agreed to the firing, it would notify the teacher. If the teacher wanted to appeal the firing, the board would set a hearing. But who was going to hear the case? It would be the school board that just fired the teacher, and that was not exactly due process.

I introduced the independent hearing officer bill in the education committee and got it passed, not only in the House but also in the Senate. This was a somewhat unusual case of legislation passing not because it was pushed by an interest group, but because it was the right thing to do.

Until then I had been a nonentity as far as the teachers unions were concerned because they didn't know what my allegiances were, IFT or IEA. Because neither of the unions had been involved with the bill, each thought that the other had supported it. Both wanted to take credit for the bill, even though they didn't know where it was coming from. When it passed and the unions discovered that I wasn't in either of their pockets, I suddenly became the darling of both groups.

However, school boards throughout the state weren't happy with the bill, and from then on I had a love-hate relationship with them. The love came in when they needed money. I got an appropriations bill passed that gave suburban Chicago school districts more funding than they ever had before. It was a big spending bill that also forgave a significant amount of debt that the Chicago Public Schools system had incurred.

Even my seatmate, Glenn Schneider, a Democrat from the western suburbs who was passionate and well-versed about public education, told me: "The state can't afford this bill. It's a Christmas-tree bill, and the governor will veto it." In a debate on the floor of the House, I said, "Glenn, you're absolutely right: This is a Christmas-tree bill, it does give everyone everything they want – and that's why the governor is going to sign it." Dan Walker was governor at the time, and sign it he did.

I became the darling of the suburban school districts because I had brought them more money than they had ever gotten before, but I had also gotten a bill passed that benefited the teachers. That's the beauty of being a loose cannon: You work for legislation that benefits the people first and try to avoid letting the interests control the day. Not going to interested parties for campaign contributions sure helps in that process. When you operate that way, the interests don't know quite what to make of you.

Change, of course, is the great constant. Most things change, and few things remain the same. Old-time precinct captains once took the pulse of their communities by going door to door, but today, in the age of the Internet, we can know what other people are thinking 24 hours a day without leaving our own homes. Media and money have changed the political landscape and have contributed to distancing the people from their politics. All of these factors are part of the continuum of American social change.

Let's consider, though, the direction in which some of these changes have taken us. That direction isn't a steady path to better; it's a slow but sure path to worse. Looking back on the way things used to be isn't a pointless exercise in nostalgia. We need to ask ourselves: Is this kind of change going to get us to where we want to go? Then having asked the question, we have to be honest with ourselves about the answers.

When I was growing up, the world was a simpler place. Today it is a lot more complex, and the role of the United States in the world is quite different. Before World War II, the United States was not the No. 1 power in the world, and we did not have the technology that we have today.

When our international standing changed after WWII, the world began to look to us for leadership, and at first we responded in a manner that was significantly different from the way other victorious nations had responded. It used to be that the country that won the war prevailed by chopping up the losing countries and taking away their riches.

But that's not what we did after WWII. We created the Marshall Plan that put our former enemies, among others, back on their feet. And because we became the predominant country in the free world and started to amass such great wealth, other countries looked to us, and we became everybody's uncle, Uncle Sam.

To be sure, before the United States began to rise to prominence on the world stage in the mid-20th century, we had engaged in conflicts on the North American continent – with Mexico, with Spain and with native Americans – that were driven as much by interests as by values, if not more so.

But as we began to assume the mantle of leader of the free world – at least for a time, however brief – we seemed to be guided by principles. Americans really believed that we should set an example for democracy and freedom. At the same time, many countries wanted to imitate the United States because we had wealth, because we were inventive, because we were ingenious and most of all, because we had freedom.

American popular culture of the time reflected this thinking, and the motion-picture industry beamed it across the land and around the world. The ideal men in our society were supposed to be like John Wayne: tall, handsome and rugged with a good heart, who always fought for the right and never did anything bad. The ideal women were just like Doris Day: more like an angel than a human being, who always came to people's rescue, who didn't have a mean bone in her body.

At the same time, our own society was experiencing conflict revolving around issues that included segregation and racial discrimination, poverty and women's rights. Still, we believed that we would always reach the right conclusion and do the right thing, and we told the world that it could always rely on us to do that.

But things changed over time, and instead of being a moral compass for the world, we became a symbol for money. Instead of upholding American values of freedom and democracy, of equal rights and opportunities, we started to lose our perspective, which was based on the American dream. We became less concerned with American values and more concerned with American interests.

Today American interests are not necessarily our interests alone. In the global economy, developed nations have become increasingly connected, and economic weakness in one can be felt across the system. More than that, American interests no longer represent what most Americans still understand to be American values. The values of the people have been supplanted by corporate interests, in many cases with the support of our own government.

On the surface we preach democracy and equal rights for all in a world at peace. For the most part, through the middle of the 20th century, our allies were countries that had the same interests that we did and shared the same democratic values, even though there were exceptions and contradictions.

While fighting the good fight of World War II, we found strange bedfellows in undemocratic allies such as Joseph Stalin and Chiang Kai-shek. Before WWII our credo was that we start no wars but fight only defensive wars when we or our allies were attacked, while in reality we made notable exceptions in places such as Cuba and the Philippines.

But for the last 60 years we have routinely aligned ourselves with nations that don't share our stated values. We have supported some of the worst dictators – Augusto Pinochet, Manuel Noriega, the Shah of Iran, Idi Amin and Hosni Mubarak, to name but a few. We have flip-flopped to support those who were once our enemies but became our friends – not for ideological reasons but because we have common expedient interests. American interests are often connected to increasing the bottom line.

This has led to a near-constant state of war. We have waged war for decades on foreign soils at great cost to American life and treasure in Korea, Vietnam and now the Middle East and south-central Asia.

Since World War II we have gone to war more often to defend our interests than to defend our values. But what are our interests – and who defines them? They have increasingly been tied to power and profit rather than to political philosophies.

And so we have fought a series of wars and established hundreds of military bases around the world. We have burdened our national resources beyond belief by creating the very military-industrial complex that Eisenhower, a revered Republican, warned us not to. But we did it anyway.

Given the way American thinking has evolved about our place in the world, it's not surprising that this thinking has also taken root at home. The money-is-power credo has become conspicuous in many aspects of American life.

We used to have the best educational system in the world, bar none. We used to have the best accessible medical system in the world. There used to be a long list of things at which we were the best, and that was because we were headed in the right direction.

We knew that all children deserved an education, because our future relies on our children. We believed that people should have access to quality medical care, that no one should go hungry, that everyone should have freedom of opportunity. But the mentality of greed has overshadowed those ideals. As the cost of college education increases, access to education diminishes. As the cost of health care increases, access to health care diminishes.

If we want to be No. 1, we have to be No. 1 for the right reasons. We must pursue the American dream that the early American philosophers envisioned even before the term "American dream" was coined: a country that is educated, a country that is free from hunger, a country that can be a beacon for the rest of the world.

To be that beacon, though, our light has to show that we are following our own ideals. When we did that, we were the people that other nations wanted to follow. But today we are not living up to our own ideals, and as a result we have fallen off our exalted pedestal.

The politicians are leading us in the wrong direction because they're following the money rather than the ideals. The American compass points to the popular saying: If you want to find out what's really happening, follow the money.

The influence of moneyed interests on the political process is as old as the republic itself. What has changed is the degree to which follow-the-money thinking dominates American politics today.

While it is a truism that the candidates who raise the most money are usually the candidates who win elections – in presidential races since 1980, the best-financed candidate won eight out of 10 contested primaries[12] – political fundraising is only the beginning of the influence of money on politics. Once in office, those elected to represent the people's interests constantly rub elbows with a virtual army of lobbyists who represent moneyed interests that jockey for influence on the policy-making process.

After Congress passed the financial reform bill in July 2010, which was hailed as the most wide-ranging overhaul of financial regulation since the New Deal, *Time* magazine reported that the scope of lobbying efforts that paralleled the legislative process was nothing short of remarkable. Approximately 2,000 registered lobbyists for the financial industry (including banks, investment houses and insurance companies) were on the job during the process – nearly four lobbyists for every member of the U.S. House and Senate.

In the House-Senate conference committee that pounded out compromise legislation, *Time* reported, "the lawmakers usually worked out the differences between the bills in secret, often inserting entirely new and undebated provisions provided at the last minute by lobbyists. The full House and Senate would then have to vote up or down on the final result, often without having had time to read, much less consider, those changes."[13]

Not only were the changes voluminous, they were complex, and according to *Time*: "Complexity is the modern lobbyist's greatest ally. The House bill was 1,615 pages; the Senate version was 1,565. The final bill weighed in at 2,319 pages. And on almost every page there were dozens of phrases – typically framed in near unintelligible legalese – whose wording could mean millions or billions to some company or industry."[14]

The 2,000 lobbyists at work on the financial reform legislation in 2010 represented a fraction of the 12,941 registered lobbyists operating that year in the nation's capital, according to the Center for Responsive Politics. A total of $3.51 *billion* was spent on lobbying in 2010, the CRP reported – more than double the $1.56 billion in lobbying expenditures in 2000, when the number of lobbyists at work in Washington, at 12,540, was only 3 percent fewer.[15]

The lobbying industry has been likened to lawyers and their clients being allowed to make donations to the jury before it decides a case.[16] Indeed, in January 2010 the influence of moneyed interests on the political process was granted an unprecedented level of privilege and legitimacy by no less esteemed an institution than the U.S. Supreme Court.

In *Citizens United v. Federal Election Commission*, the highest court in the land expanded the power of corporations and unions in the political process, allowing them to pay for "independent expenditures" – political communication that advocates the election or defeat of candidates – directly out of their treasuries rather than having to channel donations through political action committees.

Here's what the court said: "The Government may regulate corporate political speech through disclaimer and disclosure requirements, but it may not suppress that speech altogether. ... [T]he government may not suppress political speech on the basis of the speaker's corporate identity" because "[n]o sufficient governmental interest justifies limits on the political speech of nonprofit or for-profit corporations."[17]

In plain terms, this means that the Supreme Court has given corporations and unions First Amendment rights that previously had been reserved for individuals – or, in other words, real people. Despite this equal status bump, however, corporations and unions hardly have equal power when it comes to political spending.

Data compiled by the Center for Responsive Politics showed a corporate-labor donation ratio of 20:1 by the end of October 2011 in the 2011-12 election cycle. Labor groups had contributed $18.7 million to candidates, political parties, independent expenditures and electioneering communications in federal campaigns.

By contrast, corporate interests – including individual companies and industry associations in sectors including finance, insurance, communications/electronics, health, energy/natural resources, real estate, construction, agribusiness, transportation, defense and others – had contributed $374 million.[18]

The reasoning behind the high court's 5-4 ruling appeared to be based on the premise that only contributions made directly to candidates and officeholders pose a threat of quid pro quo corruption, a risk not posed by independent expenditures. However, one legal observer remarked in the *Indiana Law Review* that "narrowing the government's interest in preventing corruption has consequences that extend well beyond the regulations struck down in *Citizens United*, because virtually all campaign-finance regulation depends on this anti-corruption rationale for its constitutionality."[19]

The potentially chilling effect of *Citizens United* on future campaign-finance reform legislation is a red flag, as noted in a Harvard law journal commentary: Creating a legal framework that effectively invalidates campaign-expenditure limitations "signals the Court's newfound hostility toward campaign-finance regulation in all but the most limited of circumstances."[20]

Against this backdrop – ranging from the funding of presidential and congressional campaigns to the phalanx of lobbyists at work in Washington to the current disposition of the Supreme Court on related matters – it is no wonder that Americans have come to believe that what's good for General Motors is good for America. In other words: Whatever is good for the people with money is good for the country.

At the same time, however, the spectacle of big money's influence on the political process diminishes our sense that by participating in the system as individuals – whether by working for a political cause or candidate, or by showing up at a protest rally, or by getting out and voting – we can really change things. We have become convinced that money is power. But what about the power of the people?

American politics has morphed into a common commodity that is bought and paid for by consumers with interests. This is entirely consistent with our having evolved into a "gimme" society.

Our obsession with consumption has led many of us to believe that every home has to have three TVs, four computers, new cars. We think that every new thing is a necessity. The addictive balm of consumption diverts our attention from public affairs.

The essential link between the people and their politics has been weakened. This link is leaders who understand what the people need and how to achieve it. But when the leaders become estranged from their constituents, and the politics is no longer of the people, Americans begin to lose the sense that we can control our destiny. And that's what is happening in this country today.

By and large, people don't view politics the same way that my immigrant father did. He was born in a place where he couldn't participate in public life outside his own religious community, where he had no say. Participating in the political process as an American citizen was a big thing for my father. Being able to stand up and say what he wanted to say was *the* thing.

Over the last half century, however, there has been a gradual but fairly steady decline in national voter turnout rates. The presidential election year 1960 brought out 63.1 percent of the American voting-age population; by the presidential election year 2008, turnout had dropped to 56.8 percent.[21]

As the American people continue to be distanced from their politics, the American dream is becoming further and further out of reach for more and more Americans. If we continue to sit still and passively disengage, and if we accept the substitution of political expedience for policy and principle, then we won't be able to move forward as a society. Instead, only the privileged relatively few will prosper.

We may have already arrived at this very scenario. Consider the hue and cry of the Occupy Wall Street protestors: *"We are the 99 percent."* They remind us of the grossly inequitable gap between the top 1% of richest Americans and the rest of us in the 99 percentiles below. Implicit in the protestors' message is that our representatives should be doing more on behalf of the people who elected them.

If we do not endeavor to achieve a more equitable balance of opportunity, if we do not reclaim a politics of the people, then the world that we want, the world of the American dream, will remain beyond the grasp of generations to come.

And perhaps it will even disappear altogether.

3
No Easy Way Out

By early 2012, Americans were still suffering the effects of the Great Recession and the crash of '08. Many were struggling with unemployment and dwindling personal assets, the latter epitomized by the widespread foreclosure fiasco and a collapsed real estate market. Many recent college graduates were facing uncertain if not bleak futures in which low-paying, if any, employment and years of educational debt lie ahead.

We have been hit hard. So hard, in fact, that for the first time in more than 40 years, Americans have poured into the streets by the thousands to protest, "occupying" Wall Street and other venues across the country.

There are many threads in the fast-unraveling tapestry of the American dream, many discrete political and economic factors that have combined to bring us to this point in American history. In brief and simple terms, two major public-policy drivers that have intersected over time are at the core of the conditions we are facing today.

This narrative has an underlying theme, and that theme is no less important than the details of the narrative itself. The theme is that in public policy, as in life, the best way is not necessarily the easy way out.

No matter how admirable the goal may be, the ends rarely justify the means. If a solution to a vexing problem seems too good to be true, then most likely it is.

Those relatively few with the most to gain will apply pressure to the gatekeepers of policy, trying to get them to take the easy way out instead of finding solutions that serve the people's interests. When the gatekeepers take the easy way out, the people pay the price.

It is conventional wisdom that the economic crisis of 2008 was precipitated by bubbles in the housing and financial markets, and that those bubbles were closely linked.

The housing bubble was largely the result of federal policies aimed at increasing opportunity for home ownership; the financial bubble was associated with federal deregulation of various aspects of the commercial banking industry. Both sets of policies were imprudent, each in its own way offering the false promise of an easy way out.

The Great Depression brought Franklin Delano Roosevelt to the White House, and he instituted the New Deal. Of the myriad programs it produced, all had a common theme of security. Two new agencies implemented the New Deal's housing program: the Home Owners' Loan Corporation and the Federal Housing Administration.

The HOLC was established in 1933 primarily to protect defaulting homeowners against foreclosure and to assist banks by refinancing troubled mortgages. The FHA, which followed in 1934, was created to insure long-term mortgages the way the FDIC insured bank deposits and to define national standards for home construction. Fannie Mae (the Federal National Mortgage Association), created in 1938, provided banks with a mechanism to resell their mortgages, thus increasing the lenders' liquidity and making more money available for new home building.[1]

Decades later in 1970, Freddie Mac (the Federal Home Loan Mortgage Corporation) was created to buy mortgages on the secondary market, pool them and sell them as mortgage-backed securities to investors on the open market.[2]

These regulatory agencies broadened opportunities for Americans to own homes. Before the New Deal, approximately 40 percent lived in homes they owned; by the 1970s nearly two-thirds of Americans were homeowners. At the beginning of the 21st century, nearly 70 percent of Americans owned their own homes.[3]

In 1977 a majority Democratic Congress passed and President Carter signed the Community Reinvestment Act, whose goal was to end redlining by banks that would not offer mortgages in low-income neighborhoods with high minority concentrations.[4] Seeking to increase the homeownership rate for low- and moderate-income Americans even further, in the mid-1990s President Clinton sought to reform CRA guidelines so that "more Americans should own their own homes, for reasons that … go to the heart of what it means to harbor, to nourish and to expand the American dream." This policy took shape as the National Homeownership Strategy.[5]

As a result, banks now had to prove, through a federal testing process, that their market shares in low- and moderate-income areas equaled market shares in their overall service areas. This policy produced a likely unintended consequence: "Both banks and unregulated financial institutions devised new ways to make housing affordable by offering no-down payment, no-documentation, stated-income and adjustable-rate loans with low, teaser rates and the option to negatively amortize principal."[6]

In other words, for many of these so-called "subprime" borrowers who would otherwise not be able to qualify for mortgages and own homes, this was a government-granted easy way out.

Further facilitating the homeownership strategy, Fannie Mae and Freddie Mac, known as government sponsored entities or GSEs, were not only able to borrow money at rates just above those on U.S. Treasury securities, but they were also enabled by Clinton and the majority Democratic Congress to reduce their capital requirements to 2.5 percent, even though the requirement for commercial banks was 10 percent. Moreover, the GSEs could qualify for affordable-housing credit under the CRA by buying securities that were derived from subprime loans and converted into bonds.[7]

The aggregate effect of these favorable conditions for the GSEs, which continued through the Bush administration that followed, was to raise not only their profile but also their profitability. By 2008 Fannie and Freddie together owned or guaranteed $5 trillion of the $11 trillion U.S. housing market and were the largest purchasers of U.S. mortgages.[8]

The creation of the housing bubble intersected neatly with the creation of the financial bubble, which was fueled by deregulation. One of the hallmark pieces of New Deal legislation was the Banking Act of 1933, also known as the Glass-Steagall Act. To safeguard against future economic crashes, it prevented the formation of financial conglomerates by separating commercial and investment banking. Decades later, provisions of the Bank Holding Company Act of 1956 separated commercial banking from the insurance business.

Beginning in the era of government deregulation ushered in by the Reagan administration, from 1984 to 1997 there were 25 failed attempts to dismantle Glass-Steagall. However, by the 1990s the profits being reaped in the subprime market by the GSEs as a result of Clinton's CRA reforms accelerated this deregulatory drive. By one account, "Republicans were champing at the bit to do away" with certain provisions of Glass-Steagall and the Bank Holding Company Act "in order to break the GSEs' predominance in the securitization of mortgages, a very lucrative business."[9]

Indeed, by 1995 the subprime-loan market had reached $90 billion, and it doubled over the next three years. Moreover, complex financial instruments known as derivatives were proliferating on Wall Street. These derivatives included collateralized debt obligations, or CDOs, which pooled millions of subprime mortgages to ratchet up profits further; and credit-default swaps, which provided hedges against the default of subprime mortgages. Derivatives generated not only ever-higher profits but also increased risk throughout the financial system.[10]

Deregulation of the financial markets was also externally driven. Deregulation supporters in the White House, Congress and federal regulatory agencies wanted to ensure that the U.S. financial industry would remain competitive with its European counterparts in the post-Cold War era of a rapidly globalizing international financial system and a unifying European currency.

The charge to dismantle Glass-Steagall was led in Congress by Republican Senator Phil Gramm of Texas, and the legislation that did just that bore his name. The Gramm-Leach-Bliley Act of November 1999 collapsed the wall between commercial and investment banking, allowing single holding companies formed by financial institutions to offer banking, securities and insurance as was permitted before the Great Depression.

The demise of Glass-Steagall also had a prime advocate in the Clinton cabinet in Treasury Secretary Robert Rubin. Days before the passage of GLBA, Rubin resigned his post to accept a $40 million-a-year job at Citigroup, which had spent more than $100 million lobbying Congress for the legislation.[11]

The following year, with bipartisan support in Congress, Clinton signed the Commodity Futures Modernization Act of 2000, which shielded the derivatives market from federal regulation. In 2004, the Bush administration continued on this deregulatory path, with the Securities and Exchange Commission lowering capital requirements for the big five investment houses of Goldman Sachs, Morgan Stanley, Merrill Lynch, Lehman Brothers and Bear Stearns. By 2007 their leverage-to-capital ratios had reached 26 to 1.[12]

Liquidity crises ensued, and by April 2008 these major Wall Street firms had suffered an estimated $230 billion in proprietary trading losses on toxic assets.[13] By late fall 2008, all five had either gone bankrupt (Lehman Brothers), been taken over in mergers with larger commercial banks orchestrated by banking regulators (Bear Stearns and Merrill Lynch) or accepted massive federal bailouts and converted into bank holding companies (Goldman Sachs received a $12.9 billion payout from the government's bailout of insurance giant AIG;[14] Morgan Stanley borrowed $107.3 billion from the Fed during the crisis, more than any other bank[15]).

Bailouts of GSEs Fannie Mae and Freddie Mac were also huge, estimated by the Federal Housing Finance Agency to total $124 billion through 2014.[16]

The link between moneyed interests, legislative process and deregulation is clear and undeniable, and there is no easy way out of the resulting disaster.

The banking and financial-services industries spent $300 million to lobby Congress for the virtual repeal of the Glass-Steagall Act, according to an estimate by Joseph Stiglitz, a Nobel Prize laureate in economics and former chief economist of the World Bank.[17] Such a vast money trail would point in myriad directions, and it would connect scores of corporate interests to the campaign coffers of a multitude of our elected representatives in Congress.

A prime example of this linkage is Gramm, who served as chairman of the Senate banking committee from 1995 to 2000. *Time* magazine ranked Gramm No. 2 on its list of "25 People to Blame for the Financial Crisis" published in February 2009. *Time* gave the No. 1 spot to Angelo Mozilo, former CEO of Countrywide Financial, the mortgage lender that played a key role in the subprime debacle; the No. 3 spot went to former Federal Reserve chief Alan Greenspan.[18]

Time called Gramm "Washington's most prominent and outspoken champion of financial deregulation." In addition to his role in the repeal of Glass-Steagall, Gramm engineered an easy out for the financial industry by inserting a provision in the Commodity Futures Modernization Act of 2000 that exempted derivative instruments including credit-default swaps from regulation by the federal Commodity Futures Trading Commission. According to *Time*, by February 2009 credit-default swaps, which caused the liquidity crisis and subsequent federal bailout of AIG, had cost the U.S. $150 billion.[19]

When it passed, Gramm asserted that the commodity futures act would "protect financial institutions from overregulation" and "position our financial-services industries to be world leaders into the new century." Because the legislation also exempted energy-futures trading from regulatory oversight, it had been heavily lobbied for by Enron,[20] whose subsequent 2001 accounting scandal and bankruptcy wreaked havoc on the California energy market and lost billions for investors, employees, pensioners and creditors.

According to the Washington-based watchdog group Public Citizen, between 1989 and 2001 Gramm took $97,350 in campaign contributions from Enron, making him the energy company's second-largest congressional recipient; in 1999-2000 Enron spent $3.45 million to lobby Congress for deregulation of energy-futures trading, among other issues.[21]

Gramm's wife also cultivated a relationship with Enron. In 1992 Wendy Gramm, as chair of the Commodity Futures Trading Commission, was instrumental in pushing through an easy out for Enron – a rule that excluded its energy-futures contracts from government oversight. Within weeks of leaving the commission, she was appointed to Enron's board of directors; according to

Public Citizen, the energy giant paid her between $915,000 and $1.8 million in salary, stock options, dividends and other benefits from 1993 to 2001.[22]

When he retired from the Senate in 2002, Phil Gramm joined Swiss global financial-services giant UBS. He became vice chairman of its Investment Bank division and registered as a lobbyist in 2004. By 2007 Gramm was lobbying Congress for UBS on legislation regarding the mortgage crisis at the same time that he was serving as national campaign co-chair for Republican presidential candidate Senator John McCain.

UBS deregistered Gramm as a lobbyist in April 2008;[23] three months later he resigned from the McCain campaign. At the end of 2011, he still occupied his vice chairman post at UBS.[24]

The financial collapse of 2008 spurred not only a flurry of government bailouts but also the financial reform legislation known as the Dodd-Frank Wall Street Reform and Consumer Protection Act of 2010. In part, the reform addressed proprietary trading, a result of the repeal of Glass-Steagall that enabled banks and investment houses to make speculative investments for their own profit, paid from their own accounts.

Senators Jeff Merkley (D.-Oregon) and Carl Levin (D.-Michigan) introduced an amendment to Dodd-Frank that would ban U.S. banks from proprietary trading, which the two legislators have cited as a critical factor in the global financial crisis and subsequent recession.

"The major global financial firms' proprietary trading losses contributed significantly to the freezing of global financial markets, helping to precipitate more than $17 trillion in investment losses and necessitating bailouts by governments all over the world," the senators wrote in a Harvard journal in 2011. "While a massive economic collapse was prevented, the subsequent recession was nonetheless extraordinarily severe, and the recovery has been slow."[25]

The Merkley-Levin amendment was a key provision of the proposal by former Federal Reserve Chairman Paul Volcker that sought to ban proprietary trading. Although the senators' amendment never made it to a vote, the so-called Volcker Rule was ultimately adopted as part of Dodd-Frank, and its provisions were scheduled to take effect in July 2012.[26]

In its final form, however, the Volcker Rule includes a number of exceptions that bear the distinct imprint of lobbyists for the financial industry – 2,000 of whom were reported to have worked financial reform issues as the legislation made its way through Congress. These exceptions include exemptions for most mutual-fund companies and a provision that allows banks to manage client funds while still investing up to 3 percent of their own capital and taking up to seven years to sell off current investments. Banks are also allowed to define their capital in such a way that the 3 percent cap on their own investments is effectively increased.[27]

In addition, the financial reform act introduced new hedge-fund regulation, changed the definition of accredited investors, and required reporting on CEO to median employee pay ratios and other compensation data by all public companies. It also mandated equitable access to consumer credit and provided incentives to promote banking among low-income and medium-income earners.[28]

Dodd-Frank has been heralded as nothing less than a sweeping overhaul of the rules and regulations that govern the U.S. financial industry, landmark legislation to ensure that banks no longer become so big that a collapse could threaten the global financial system and force taxpayers to bail them out. But some argue that the reform legislation does not go far enough, in part because it does not reinstate the strict separation between commercial and investment banking that Glass-Steagall provided.

To address this and other shortcomings of Dodd-Frank, in April 2011 Rep. Marcy Kaptur (D.-Ohio) introduced H.R. 1489, the Return to Prudent Banking Act, which would repeal certain provisions of the Gramm-

Leach-Bliley Act of 1999 and reinstate the banking-investment separation of the Glass-Steagall Act of 1933.

"We have suffered the largest transfer of wealth from Main Street to Wall Street through both the housing crisis and the financial crisis," Kaptur wrote on her congressional website. "The six largest banks ... now hold over two-thirds of our nation's assets." Among other reasons Dodd-Frank did not go far enough, according to Kaptur, is that it did not reform credit-rating agencies, require transparent derivatives trading on an exchange, end too big to fail and encourage prudent lending.[29]

The irony of government compliance in the deregulation of the U.S. financial industry is inescapable, and its folly came full circle in 2011. As the one-year anniversary of Dodd-Frank approached, Thomas Hoenig, president of the Kansas City Federal Reserve, gave a speech that June in which he called banks that are too big to fail "fundamentally inconsistent with capitalism" and "inherently destabilizing to global markets and detrimental to world growth."

As long as the concept of SIFIs, or systemically important financial institutions, exists "and there are institutions so powerful and considered so important that they require special support and different rules," Hoenig said, "the future of capitalism is at risk and our market economy is in peril."[30]

Action against those alleged to have committed white-collar crimes that spurred the near-collapse of the economy also began to emerge. In September the Federal Housing Finance Agency, which regulates Fannie Mae and Freddie Mac, sued 17 financial institutions over the toxic mortgage bonds they sold to the two federal mortgage giants during the housing bubble. Targets of the lawsuits filed in federal and state courts included Bank of America, Citigroup, Countrywide Financial, Goldman Sachs, JPMorgan Chase, Merrill Lynch and Morgan Stanley.

The suits alleged that all of the institutions had been negligent in misrepresenting the risks embedded in securities backed by subprime mortgages and other risky loans; some institutions were also alleged to have committed fraud. Damage demands were not disclosed but were estimated in billions of dollars. The FHFA had filed a similar lawsuit in July against Swiss bank UBS to recoup losses of more than $900 million.[31]

In December 2011 six former Fannie and Freddie executives were named in a lawsuit filed by the Securities and Exchange Commission, which alleged that they had misled investors over exposure to risky home loans.[32]

And so, a perfect storm hovers above the American dream: The policy makers have opted for easy ways out, with the moneyed interests having greased the wheels. Regulations that safeguarded the public interest have been dealt a severe blow, and we are still trying to recover from the resulting chaos.

For the past seven years, I have assumed the role of a regulator in Illinois state government. It was not a role that I sought; it was one for which I was sought out. As chairman of the Illinois Gaming Board, which regulates casino and video gaming in the state, I have had the opportunity to preside over a process that in some ways mirrors our American predicament.

My bird's-eye view of the regulatory process on the state level has made all the more clear to me the logic of the troubles that we are facing on the national level. The scope and details of the two scenarios are different, of course. However, the underlying patterns are similar.

In February 2005 I was barely two months into retirement from 20 years on the bench as a Cook County Circuit Court judge. I was also just three months away from my 75th birthday. Charlotte and I were enjoying the beautiful weather and Pacific coast scenery of La Jolla, California, on a break from the cold and bleak Chicago winter, when a phone call came from Chicago. It was the office of the governor of Illinois, Rod Blagojevich, asking if I would accept an appointment to become chairman of the Illinois Gaming Board.

State-sponsored gaming started in Illinois in the 1990s. I get a kick out of calling it gaming – in actuality it is gambling with the "bl" taken out. Riverboat gambling had taken root in Iowa, just across the Mississippi River. Some downstate legislators (in Illinois, locales beyond Cook County and the five surrounding "collar" counties are considered downstate) saw these riverboat casinos popping up in Iowa and said: Let's do it in Illinois to fund public education.

The legislature enacted the Riverboat Gambling Act in February 1990, making Illinois the second state after Iowa to legalize riverboat gambling. The first Illinois riverboat casino began operating in Alton on the Mississippi in September 1991.

The law stipulated that casinos could not be located in Chicago off Lake Michigan, however, and that the extent of gaming would be limited to 10 riverboat casinos throughout the state. The first Illinois Gaming Board was constituted as a regulatory body that would, among other functions, determine the locations of the 10 riverboat casinos. Each location required a company that wanted to operate a boat there and a municipal or county government that wanted a boat within its jurisdiction.

Legalizing gambling to raise revenues for public education is an easy choice but not necessarily good public policy. When a state resorts to raising money for education by promoting gambling, it appears that the state is saying: "Let's not really look at how to solve our problems. Let's do something under the radar that everyone will accept." This is the expedient thing to do, but it will not solve our revenue problems in the long term. To solve these problems, there is no easy way out.

Gambling can become an addiction, and when it does, it is a disease. It can ruin families and strip them of their assets. The gaming industry is constantly creating new and different ways to gamble, but the public doesn't have sufficient information about the possible consequences of gambling or how to address those consequences when they occur.

We have come a long way since the original one-armed bandit – you put a coin in it, threw a lever and three wheels would spin. If they stopped in a certain combination, you won. Computer technology has changed the nature of gambling entirely. Today video gambling machines provide dozens of ways to bet. Moreover, casinos are glitzy places with lots of lights and noise but without windows and clocks. These settings shut out the outside world and distort people's sense of reality.

Despite my reservations about the wisdom and correctness of funding public education by taxing state-sanctioned gambling, I accepted the appointment to become chairman of the Illinois Gaming Board. I accepted it because I have never believed that one should sit on the sidelines and *kvetch*, the term my father would use for complaining. If you have an opportunity to do something, you do it.

When Gov. Blagojevich called, there was a lot of public complaining going on about the Illinois Gaming Board, which had all sorts of clouds hanging over it. Three of its five members had resigned, and the board had not met for seven months. It was behind in its work, and people were upset that it wasn't operating very well.

More than that, gaming in Illinois had gotten on the public radar, but not in a good way. The board had issued a license for a casino on the Mississippi River near Galena that had now become the subject of controversy. The Emerald Casino company, which held the license, believed that the casino wasn't meeting financial expectations and wanted to relocate it and sell the use of the license.

The legislature passed a bill permitting the transfer of the license, and the prior gaming board then approved the transfer along with relocation of the casino to Rosemont, which abuts O'Hare airport. This, in turn, prompted allegations of improper outside influence on the board's decision-making process. If that weren't enough, a full-blown scandal ensued when Emerald principals attempted to skirt gaming-board protocol, prompting calls for the license to be revoked.

To resolve the matter, the new IGB – Blagojevich eventually appointed four other new members along with me – had to examine the situation and hold the matter up to public scrutiny.

So our first action was to ask Abner Mikva, the respected jurist, to act as administrative law judge in the matter. We thought that he would be the ideal person to review the facts of the case and make recommendations about the revocation of the license.

Mikva accepted the commission. After holding several months of extensive hearings in 2005, he concluded that the license should be revoked. The gaming board reviewed his recommendation and concurred with it. We voted to revoke the license.

And so began my work as chair of the Illinois Gaming Board. As a judge I never liked to preside over cases in which others made the decisions. I like to make the call, and if I'm wrong, I'm wrong. At least I have my shot at hitting the ball.

My first call was to bring in Ab Mikva to assist us in getting gaming in Illinois back on track, and it proved to be right. So did my hunch that this was an opportunity to put my imprint on something important – safeguarding the public interest as a regulator of an industry that, despite its ability to generate revenue, is not without social risk.

State-sanctioned gambling has been billed by some legislators as an easy solution to the state's dire revenue problems. But what seems to be the easy way out is not really the easy way out.

We have to make some painful choices. Illinois had one of the lowest individual income-tax rates in the country at 3 percent, which was raised only after 28 years in 2011. We have had one of the highest sales-tax ranges, and more local governments and special taxing districts have been created in Illinois than in any other state in the nation.

Shortfalls in funding for education and public-employee pensions as well as in other areas of social spending result from our revenue pie being too small to divide so many ways. Gaming is a quick-fix solution for raising a significant amount of revenue because legislators are loath to increase taxes. Instead the state sanctions gambling in order to tax it while continuing to borrow money, which means that a large part of the budget must go to servicing debt.

We are not looking at the big picture. Simply put, income taxes are assessed inequitably, and the rates are inadequate to fund our basic social needs. Corporations and people with higher incomes pay proportionally less in taxes than people with lower incomes. A person with a lower income who spends more of it on necessities pays a larger proportion in taxes than a person with a higher income who spends less of it on necessities.

That's plain and simple math, but the solution is not simple politics. When I served in the Illinois House, I told my fellow legislators that the way they debated and voted on tax issues indicated that they thought their constituents would view any tax increase for any reason as a hanging offense.

The tone of their debates also envisioned an electorate that has little compassion and scorns social programs that assist the less fortunate. The only logical conclusion to be drawn from such a scenario is that legislators can never vote for an income-tax increase or vote to restructure the tax system to make it more equitable without getting thrown out of office.

I never believed that the electorate, as a whole, thinks this way. No one likes to pay taxes, and we all want to keep more of what we earn in our own pockets. But people also understand that we need public education, unemployment compensation, pensions and health care – and that we have to pay for them.

However, policy makers often resort to expedience to meet those needs. This has typically meant not raising taxes outright but taxing things that few object to being taxed for, which include gambling, alcohol and tobacco. Taxes on these are sin taxes, and sin taxes are expedient.

Hidden taxes, such as the ones embedded in our telephone and other utility bills, are also expedient. The taxes that are not expedient are right out front: income tax, sales tax and property tax. You see those taxes every time you pay them.

Deciding what to tax and at what rate is a kind of shell game. We play the game and think that we have solved the revenue problem, but we haven't.

Illinois and other states are in the gambling business because it is expedient. The state looks the other way on the morality of the issue, and the public as a whole doesn't object to the state taxing gambling because we need the revenue it brings. Illinois riverboat casinos have typically generated between $500 million and $800 million a year, which supplements funding for public education.

The Illinois Gaming Board regulates operation of casinos and video gaming, and the regulation is extensive and complex. The gaming board is tasked with ensuring the integrity of gaming – but that's a bit of an oxymoron. Gambling is not a moral activity, and the odds always favor the house.

Casinos are similar to banks because casinos do a lot of things that banks do. They both deal with money, so they have to be monitored and their actions must be subject to regulation. In a casino, wins that exceed a certain amount have to be recorded and reported to the federal government for tax and other purposes. The purpose of the regulation is to keep state-sanctioned gambling out of the reach of criminal elements. The bottom line is to protect the public.

Every inch of every casino except the restrooms is under video surveillance by the casinos at all times, and the gaming board also uses the surveillance for its purposes. If a dispute arises between a gambler and a dealer, the video enables the IGB to determine what really happened. In one case a gambler played a table game and maintained that he had double-bet a hand. But the dealer said no, he hadn't.

When we looked at the video, it was obvious that the gambler hadn't double-bet but had tried to slip in an extra chip. He bet on two blackjack hands at once, lost on one hand and then tried to push another chip onto the winning hand to double his winnings there. But the video images didn't lie. To keep criminal activity away from the casinos, IGB agents and state police must be ever alert.

The Illinois Gaming Board licenses all casino employees, everyone from the general manager to those who do the most routine maintenance jobs. The board checks everyone's background, including criminal records, to prevent people who have ties to criminal elements from working in or otherwise being connected to the casinos. Even casino employees who are not executives or in direct contact with customers can attempt illegal activity in concert with someone else.

The IGB also does background checks on many of the people and companies that provide services for the casinos, including gambling-machine manufacturers. Slot machines are run by computer chips. Those computer chips have to be tested in an independent lab that is operated exclusively for gaming regulators to make sure that the chips aren't compromised. The board also does background checks on shareholders who own more than a certain percentage of casino companies.

Gaming-board revenue agents and state police are present in all of the casinos, which can't operate without them. The casinos can't even open a slot machine to change a chip without an IGB agent there. When new chips are placed into the computer, they are protected by IGB tape, and the tape can be broken only when the chips are replaced. If a machine is opened, and the tape covering the chips has been compromised, then the casino is in trouble.

The IGB also offers self-exclusion programs for habitual and other problem gamblers. Often accompanied by family members, these gamblers register voluntarily to be excluded from entry to the casinos. By doing so they agree that if they enter it will be considered trespass and they can be arrested. If by chance such gamblers do slip into casinos and win, the self-exclusion agreement stipulates that they will forfeit their winnings and donate them to a nonprofit organization of their choice that assists problem gamblers.

Despite signing these agreements voluntarily, problem gamblers do try to get into casinos using false IDs. Casinos don't succeed in keeping all problem gamblers out. The IGB works with the casinos to prevent underage people from entry, and our agents monitor the casinos to make sure that the house doesn't take advantage of its patrons.

I was appointed chairman of the gaming board by Rod Blagojevich, but my relationship with him was rather strange: I didn't know him personally and had never met him. Two months after I took up my post, the *Chicago Tribune* published an editorial that noted Blagojevich had not met with me, despite my recent appointment or the gaming board's "crucial mission to police the integrity of Illinois casinos."

The *Tribune* wrote that Blagojevich had extended "not so much as a 'Hey' or 'Howdy,' let alone a pep talk or discussion of goals and direction."[33] And so it went: Blagojevich never called, and during the nearly four years that he was governor and I was chairman, we never met or even had a single conversation.

At the time of my appointment, the Illinois Gaming Board was part of the Department of Revenue and was dependent on it for budget and staffing. Revenue is a large agency, and the IGB was one of many units under its jurisdiction.

The board believed that it should be independent, because the IGB had to go through too much bureaucracy to operate efficiently. So we introduced our own legislation to become an independent agency. We didn't ask for Blagojevich's support or approval because we had no rapport with him.

While our bill languished in the legislature, Blagojevich left office amid a scandal that reverberated far beyond Illinois. The governor was charged with having tried to sell the state's U.S. Senate seat vacated by Barack Obama when he was elected president in November 2008. In June 2011 Blagojevich would be convicted of federal corruption charges.

Pat Quinn, who was lieutenant governor, succeeded Blagojevich as governor in early 2009. As lieutenant governor Quinn had been supportive of the gaming board. After becoming governor he proclaimed the gaming board to be an independent agency, and the state legislature acquiesced to this act of gubernatorial fiat.

I had known Quinn for a long time through Democratic Party politics in Illinois. Shortly after he became governor, I called him and said: I'm chairman of the gaming board, and I think I should sit down with you because it's a high-profile agency that the media cover closely. I think you should know what's going on.

Quinn was cordial, but having taken office amid a political firestorm, he told me: I'd love to do that. But I'm in over my head right now; things are coming at me fast and furious. He suggested that our top staff members meet first and we would meet later.

So in early 2009, along with my top administrators, I met with Quinn's people on more than one occasion. We found them to be receptive and easy to communicate with. After that I continued to try to meet with Quinn, but he had his hands full with the environment created by Blagojevich's departure and the state's fiscal crisis. With these factors at the forefront of the new governor's thinking, the gaming board did not top his priority list.

The recession plaguing the U.S. economy was at its depths. The state's deficit – topping $13 billion – had never been higher. The legislature had given Quinn a clear signal that it would not pass an income-tax increase. On top of all this, the state needed an estimated $31 billion in revenues to repair roads, bridges, schools and transit systems.

To fund this massive public-works program, in July 2009 Quinn signed into law the Video Gaming Act, which the legislature had passed just weeks before. The new law legalized video poker and other types of video gaming for all establishments (bars and restaurants) that have licenses to serve liquor on the premises. These establishments number an estimated 10,000 to 15,000 locations across the state in addition to the existing riverboat casinos.

The math of the Video Gaming Act works this way: The legislature mandated the state's revenue share at 30 percent and projected that when fully operational across the state, video gaming would yield $300 million a year in revenues. The state sells bonds to finance the public-works program. The revenues from video gaming would not finance the construction projects directly but rather service the debt they incurred.

But the $31 billion public-works price tag and the $1 billion revenue projection were illusory. When examined closely, the math changes – but few seemed to question that. Between debt service, economic downturns, and communities and counties opting out of video gaming, the Video Gaming Act could bring in considerably less than legislators had projected, and their estimates had been disputed by opponents of this gaming expansion.

According to the gaming act, the remaining 70 percent of revenues, which according to the legislature's estimate would total $700 million a year, would be split equally between video game operators and owners of establishments in which the machines are located.

Despite its promise of hundreds of millions of new revenue dollars, the Video Gaming Act would effectively transform legalized gambling in Illinois from manageable regulatory proportions to a new gaming landscape of such breadth that maintaining its integrity through regulation would become a gargantuan task. The new law virtually created a new industry. The IGB would need an exponentially larger force of agents to monitor the thousands of establishments that would be eligible for licenses, with each location allowed up to five video gambling machines.

When the legislature passed the Video Gaming Act, it did so without appropriating any funds for the gaming board to begin to put new regulations in place. It wasn't until several months later during its next session that the legislature appropriated about $4.5 million so we could start hiring new staff to draft rules, draw up licenses and establish the bidding process for a central computer system.

Prior to the new law, any slot machine or video poker machine operating outside the casinos that was used for gambling was illegal. So-called "amusement machines" in bars, restaurants and clubs were supposed to be used purely for entertainment, not gambling. But thousands of these machines went beyond that: You bet, and if you won, they paid.

That was unregulated gambling, and it was illegal. The IGB didn't know who was operating these machines and what agreements had been made between the parties, because nothing was reported. The new video gaming law provided that the IGB would now regulate the gambling machines that would pay out in thousands of establishments across the state. The gaming board would have to license tens of thousands of people to ensure that criminal elements could not penetrate the system at any one of its many entry points.

The board licenses the manufacturers, and this requires making sure they're financially sound and operating legally, with no connections to criminal elements. The IGB also licenses the distributors and then the operators, whom the law defines as the owners of the gambling machines. Operators go to the owners of bars and restaurants and make deals to place the machines in these locations.

But here's the catch: Under the law a manufacturer of a video gambling machine cannot be an operator and cannot negotiate to put its machines into an establishment. This creates an extra layer of people who profit from operation of the machines. In essence these people control the gambling-machine world, and their lobbyists have exerted considerable influence on the drafting of and push for legislation to expand gambling in Illinois.

The IGB also licenses the owners of the establishments that have gambling machines in them. The board licenses the technicians who install and maintain the machines and the handlers who transport them.

The regulation doesn't stop at licensing. It continues with monitoring and reporting on the activity of the video gambling machines. Each machine is a sophisticated computer that records players' bets, wins and losses. Each of these machines must also have the capability to be connected to a central computer system that monitors gaming activity throughout the state at all times.

Thus the Video Gaming Act would not simply turn illegal gambling machines and existing amusement machines into legal machines that the state could just license and tap for revenue. None of these machines was equipped to be connected to a central computer system; before the law was passed, a system that could monitor such a large number of gaming positions throughout the state didn't even exist.

The central computer system tells the state how much money is being taken in, how much money is disbursed in winnings and how much tax revenue the state is entitled to. Each video gambling machine also has to be equipped so that the central computer knows when the machine is opened up for collections or any other reason.

Despite these complexities, the legislature and Quinn, who as lieutenant governor had publicly expressed reservations about state-sanctioned gambling, were focused on the potential for revenue. But they had little or no understanding of what it would take to regulate the new industry that they were creating.

The amount of consultation that the legislature had with the IGB before passing the Video Gaming Act was absolute zero. Legislators were scrounging around for sources of revenue and became convinced that this was a masterful way to get it – a relatively easy way out, or so they thought, of the fiscal jam the state is in.

Legislators passed the Video Gaming Act having done no solid research, without a solid basis of revenue projection and no knowledge of what it would cost to implement. They passed it without appropriating funds for the new regulatory process that it would require.

After they passed it, I started getting calls from legislators who had voted for the bill. They asked me: How much revenue will this bring in? And I said: I don't know. Why didn't you research this before voting for it?

They passed it because they wanted money fast. The governor wanted an income-tax increase, and as painful as that would be, especially given the economic climate, he was right. But the legislators said: No tax hike, because we might not get re-elected.

And they passed the Video Gaming Act because the gaming industry told them that this was their way out of the hole. Among the video game operators' lobbyists in Springfield, one in particular stood out among the pack.

Joe Berrios has worn many hats in Illinois politics. He served three terms in the Illinois House of Representatives. He worked his way up the ladder of Cook County politics to become chairman of the Cook County Democratic Organization, a nonpaying job but a highly influential one. In addition to being elected three times as a commissioner on the Cook County Board of Review, which handles real estate tax appeals, Berrios was the Democrats' pick to run for Cook County assessor in 2010.

At the same time, Berrios was also a paid lobbyist for the Illinois Coin Machine Operators Association, which represents the video game operators in the state. By virtue of his political connections, Berrios was at the forefront of the lobby that prevailed on the legislature to pass the Video Gaming Act. Not shy about his role as a lobbyist, Berrios touted it while running for assessor. In a campaign news release, he said:

"I'm pleased that I could help get this bill passed during such a difficult fiscal time. At a time when the state is struggling for revenue, this measure will bring in $250 million to $500 million a year for use in state capital projects like roads and school construction. It's a win-win for the state.

"Our unemployment rate is at an all-time high and our schools are crumbling," Berrios continued. "This new revenue will help in so many ways. ... Once I become assessor I will resign as a lobbyist, and my sole priority will be serving the people of Cook County with fairness and efficiency."[34]

Taking note, the *Chicago Tribune* observed: "Where but Illinois can you find a candidate for public office crowing about his success as a lobbyist, working hard to bring gambling to your neighborhood?"[35] Berrios won his bid for assessor.

After passing the Video Gaming Act, the legislature turned to the gaming board and said: Make it work, and make it quick. And we replied: We'll try to do it, but you're not going to get your money quickly, because this is a complicated job.

The governor signed the legislation into law in July, and it set a September deadline for the gaming board to create new rules for video gaming. When we pointed out that it would be impossible to do a thorough job in such a short time frame, legislators backed off, but they remained impatient about moving the process forward as fast as possible.

It took the gaming board several months just to start hiring people. To write the rules and start the licensing and bidding processes, the IGB had to create new staff positions. In order to do that, it had to go through three different government agencies and consult with AFSCME, the state employees' union.

Meanwhile, in August 2009, a month after the Video Gaming Act became law, a lawsuit was filed claiming that the act contained too many disparate provisions and violated the single-subject rule of the Illinois Constitution. The case went all the way up to the state Supreme Court, which upheld the law in a July 2011 ruling.

During the two years that the case was pending, it would have been folly to issue licenses until there was no doubt that the Video Gaming Act would in fact be upheld. So by the end of 2011, nearly two and a half years after the act became law, the IGB had created the licenses and started the application process for manufacturers, distributors, suppliers and operators of the machines. But applications had not been issued for the actual video gaming locations or for the technicians or handlers.

The first round of bidding on the central computer system had been slowed by repeated objections raised by a competitor; the second round had been completed, and a contract was in the works. However, building the system would take another six months to a year.

Beyond the sheer complexities of putting the Video Gaming Act in play, there did not seem to be much public demand for it. In fact, there was public pushback.

The legislature had put a provision into the bill that local governments could opt out – and many did. Within a month of Quinn's signing the act into law on July 13, 2009, counties and communities began to opt out. As the regulators who had not been consulted before the *fait* of the Video Gaming Act had become *accompli*, the gaming board took note of the negative public reaction that quickly emerged.

On Aug. 11 the DuPage County Board, representing the state's second-largest county, which includes upper-income western suburbs that trend politically conservative, voted unanimously to ban video gaming in unincorporated areas. After the vote, board chairman Robert Schillerstrom said at a news conference that "DuPage County's quality of life is not for sale" – even though it was estimated that the ban would cost the county $300,000 in tax revenues each year.

The DuPage County Board's take on video gaming was unambiguous. Schillerstrom said, "We would encourage other communities throughout the state that it's not right for families and that it's not right for their communities." Board member Brien Sheahan zeroed in on the philosophical nut of the issue, telling reporters that "funding public works with gambling is bad public policy."36

The City Council of Evanston, a liberal college town just north of Chicago on the shore of Lake Michigan, voted unanimously to ban video gaming on Sept. 14, with Mayor Elizabeth Tisdahl saying that "the social consequences would be devastating."37 Cook County Commissioner Bridget Gainer had voiced the same sentiment in the wake of the DuPage County vote: "Every time [more gambling] is introduced," she said, "there are double-digit increases in crime and double-digit increases in personal bankruptcy and other social costs."38

By September 2010, 73 communities – most of them in the Chicago suburbs of Cook County and the surrounding five collar counties – had voted to ban video gaming in their jurisdictions, and four counties in the Chicago area had also opted out for their unincorporated areas.39

Widespread opt-outs posed a threat to the magnitude of video gaming revenues that the legislature had envisioned, in particular because the majority of opt-outs were coming from communities in Cook and the surrounding counties, which together account for two-thirds of the state's population.

Reaction from lawmakers was swift. As the opt-out momentum was gaining steam, an IGB staffer attended a legislative committee meeting in Springfield in December 2009, only to be subjected to a tongue-lashing and a plea by Rep. Angelo Saviano of the western suburbs. The *Chicago Tribune* published an editorial in February 2010 titled "Video poker extortion" that reported Saviano's remarks, which did not belie legislators' frustration.

"[From] some of the stuff you read in the newspapers and in the editorials," Saviano had said, "we feel that certain gaming board members or their designees are talking to them, giving them information, to stall [the rollout of video gambling]."

According to the *Tribune*, Saviano implored: "We have an immense amount of pressure on us to get this capital bill up and running. So if you could relay a message [to the gaming board]: Could they just keep their mouths shut and get the job done? We need this capital bill. ... And for them to keep fueling the fire with the newspapers trying to get communities [to opt] out of this is a crime."[40]

In fact, however, the gaming board had exerted no influence whatsoever on communities to opt out. This was a naturally occurring phenomenon based entirely on local opposition to video gaming. Feeling their constituents' heat, legislators passed the buck of blame on to the IGB.

In the same editorial, the *Tribune* reported that legislators were also resorting to "squeeze" tactics to persuade communities not to opt out. Saviano had cosponsored a House bill that would ban funding of capital projects with revenues from video gaming in locales that opted out. A bill introduced in the state Senate would impose a penalty on each community that opted out; the surcharge would equal the estimated revenue that the maximum allowable number of machines would have generated for the state if the community hadn't banned video gaming. Neither bill was passed.

The *Tribune* also reported that several lawmakers in Springfield warned the chair of the Kane County Board legislative committee that her county could lose state funding for capital projects unless it overturned its opt-out vote, taken in December 2009. In May 2010 Kane County, northwest of Chicago, opted back in and reversed itself on video gaming.[41]

Berrios' work as a lobbyist on behalf of the Illinois Coin Machine Operators Association did not end with the Video Gaming Act of 2009. The *Tribune* reported that he continued to lobby the legislature,[42] and in May 2010 it passed a bill that widened the scope of legalized video gaming even further to include veterans halls and truck stops. The Illinois House and Senate passed this new legislation even before a single license had been issued for legal operation of video gambling machines in bars and restaurants according to the original 2009 act.

The 2010 expansion bill contained another crucial provision that would clearly limit the power of the IGB to withhold licenses to establishments for the operation of video gambling machines.

According to the bill, the gaming board would be able to withhold licenses from applicants who had operated video gambling machines before December 2009 – only if they had been convicted of a felony for doing so. But finding a conviction for operating an illegal video gambling machine in Illinois would be like finding a needle in a haystack; there have been very few such convictions, if any.

Before the Video Gaming Act became law in 2009, thousands of video gambling machines were being operated in bars, restaurants and veterans halls across the state. The exact extent of this illegal activity was not known to the gaming board, though, because it went unreported.

When the legislature passed the Video Gaming Act, it asked the IGB to write rules and regulations. So we wrote a rule saying that anyone who continued to operate video gambling machines illegally after December 2009 would not be eligible to apply for a license to operate legally.

However, those who had ceased illegal operation before that date would have their applications reviewed on a case-by-case basis. In other words, we gave notice to those who had committed criminal activity: Stop by this date, and it will be possible for you to turn legit.

But, in fact, virtually all illegal operation of video gambling machines continued – and the expansion bill would effectively override the IGB's regulatory authority and give blanket amnesty to those who had engaged in this criminal activity. By this, the legislature showed total disregard for the law that had been in effect before passage of the Video Gaming Act.

This was Topic No. 1 on the agenda when I finally did meet with Quinn on July 30, 2010, at his office in the Thompson Center in Chicago. We met so I could explain the IGB's position on the provision in the expansion bill that would diminish the board's regulatory authority.

Quinn was running for his first elected term as governor, and the election was three months away. I could see that he was conflicted about the matter.

On the one hand, he appeared to understand our position, which was that he should amendatorily veto that portion of the bill. On the other hand, the governor explained to me that he had been getting a lot of pressure from veterans halls not to veto the bill, because many had been operating the machines on their premises. Quinn had always been supportive of veterans and service members on active duty, and he didn't want to do anything that would offend them.

The governor clearly was between the proverbial rock and a hard place. During the course of the meeting it became obvious to me that with the election looming, he might likely be inclined to make a political decision – and if he did, he might take heat for it. Not to issue an amendatory veto would be bad campaign strategy, as Quinn would be rapped by the media and groups including the Chicago Crime Commission, which were not going to look kindly on his signing this gaming expansion bill into law.

When I left, I didn't know whether he was going to sign the bill or veto it. I held out hope that he would veto it, because I thought that he understood the IGB's position and was sympathetic to it. But within a few hours of our meeting – and after the close of business that day – Quinn signed the bill.

It was a clear-cut case of politics trumping public policy. It was a clear-cut case of lobbyists influencing legislation. As a regulator charged with protecting the public interest, I was not alone in these sentiments: Within days, both the *Sun-Times* and *Tribune* came out against the governor's action. Both newspapers made direct reference to lobbyist Berrios' political connections and his influence on the process, and both lamented the potential harm that could result from this latest video gaming law.

Under the headline "Why would we cut the mob in?" the *Sun-Times* editorialized: "With legislation that Gov. Quinn signed Friday to amend the 2009 Video Gaming Act, Illinois is playing a long shot: that organized crime won't creep into the newly authorized video gaming industry. ... The new law welcomes into the new video gaming industry people who have been operating illegal video poker games in taverns all along. Not surprisingly, seeing that what they have been doing is illegal, many of these people are close associates of the mob. ... It doesn't look like we've dealt ourselves a very good hand."[43]

Under the headline "The bad guys won," the *Tribune* editorialized: "The new law was written by lobbyists for the coin-machine industry and hustled through the General Assembly without input from citizens or regulators. ... It's terrible public policy, and the governor knows it. But the bad guys have friends, and they won."[44]

At year's end, the Chicago News Cooperative asserted: "One need not be a finger-wagging bluenose to be doubtful about video gambling. ... Illinois is encouraging an industry that preys mainly on the poor, inspires addictive behavior and crime, lures the same bad guys who make money off illegal machines and perhaps does not even generate the anticipated revenue, especially with gaming down nationwide and with cities and towns around the state already putting in bans."[45]

Nonetheless, Quinn's nod to the veterans on the gaming issue may have made a crucial difference. He won his first elected term as governor in November 2010 by the narrowest of margins, beating his Republican opponent by a fraction of 1 percent of the vote.

Illinois government is in crisis mode. We have arrived at a situation of huge deficit and high unemployment. Since the Video Gaming Act was passed in 2009, joblessness in the state has ranged from 8.7 to 11.2 percent.[46] Infrastructure is crumbling; there are critical revenue shortfalls.

Prior to the 2010 election, Quinn advocated raising personal income taxes from 3 percent to 4.5 percent, but the legislature said no. It was only *after* the election that the governor and Democratic legislators in January 2011 pushed through an even larger personal income-tax hike to 5 percent and a corporate income-tax increase from 4.8 percent to 7 percent. But these increases had a political time stamp on them, with personal income taxes scheduled to drop to 3.75 percent just after the 2014 election.[47]

At the time of the income-tax hike, Illinois' combined pension and debt burden translated to $6,692 per person, the fifth-highest in the country; Moody's rated the state's general obligation bonds, which had been downgraded several times, at A1 with a negative outlook, the lowest among the 50 states.[48]

The deficit that had been reported at $15 billion at the beginning of 2011 – the income-tax hike and a four-year 2 percent government spending cap notwithstanding[49] – was projected at $5 billion by June 2012; unpaid contractors' bills, business tax refunds, Medicaid payments and employee health insurance bills were projected at an additional $8.3 billion.[50]

Because Illinois will have to borrow billions more to meet these obligations, the state's debt will only grow in the short term, and most of it will have to be serviced using revenue needed for day-to-day operation of departments and programs that serve the people. The larger the debt, the deeper in the hole we get.

Against this bleak fiscal backdrop, in May 2011 the legislature passed yet another bill – the third in less than two years – that would expand gaming in Illinois to an unprecedented degree. The measure authorized five new casinos throughout the state, including one in Chicago, and slot machines behind security areas at the two Chicago airports and at racetracks throughout the state.

A chief legislative supporter of the measure indicated not only that it could generate $1.5 billion in upfront licensing fees for the state and an additional $500 million a year in revenues, but also that Chicago Mayor Rahm

Emanuel had been "personally involved" in support of the bill, and most legislators whom he had lobbied by telephone had voted for it.[51]

Before Emanuel took office, there had been a push to bring legalized video gaming to Chicago. A coalition of business and labor groups known as "Back to Work Illinois" turned out hundreds of supporters at City Hall in April 2010 to ask the City Council to overturn the ban on video gaming. Bringing it to downtown hotels and restaurants, they argued, would save more than 130,000 jobs and deter tourists from traveling the short distance to Indiana, whose casinos reach across the state line to provide easy shuttle access.[52]

The 400-page 2011 gaming expansion bill, however, had many flaws. The measure, which had the potential to more than triple gaming capacity in Illinois,[53] would require a doubling of the Illinois Gaming Board staff to regulate.

The bill would create new gaming boards in Chicago and Springfield to oversee local gambling venues without setting precise boundaries between those agencies and the IGB. City Hall would regulate many aspects of the Chicago casino, but the Illinois State Police (which has jurisdiction over all other casinos in the state) would have no role.

Moreover, the bill required the IGB to issue provisional licenses for video gambling establishments before the board could complete criminal background checks. The measure also complicated the issue of whether the gaming board or the state racing board would have ultimate authority to require fingerprints for criminal background checks at the proposed "racinos" – racetracks with slot machines.

I pointed out these flaws in several media interviews, going so far as to say (and be repeatedly quoted) about the bill: "You can't make perfume out of a pile of garbage."

This wasn't a critique of the policy decision to expand gambling. It was about the bill hindering the IGB's ability to carry out its regulatory duties, in the public interest and with respect to the public trust.

The *Tribune* took legislators to task for their disregard for regulatory authority, opining that they failed to understand that "word of a crime problem at any Illinois casino would immediately drive away gamblers, devastate the industry statewide – and choke the revenue stream that last year poured $466 million into state and local government treasuries."[54]

Quinn came out against the bill, and legislators were fearful that he would veto it. So rather than send it to him, they prepared a new version of the legislation that was similar but, they claimed, addressed Quinn's objections. But in fact many of the problematic features of the original bill remained.

When supporters tried to push the new bill through the House in November 2011, the measure failed by a 58-53 vote. Two weeks later Quinn's office released a study it had commissioned that reported the expansion would net far less annual revenue than the $1 billion supporters had claimed – closer, rather, to $160 million for the state and $139 million for Chicago.[55] With these figures in hand, Quinn told legislators he was ready to negotiate.

Proper regulation of the state gaming industry, it seems, would be a casualty not only of legislators' desperate hunt for new revenue to ease the state's dire financial straits but also of the tailwind created by the moneyed interests that pushed legislators' buttons by fortifying their war chests.

Following the November House vote, the *Sun-Times* editorialized that Quinn had "yet to offer a convincing political argument" that the bill he said he would sign – without slot machines at racetracks and other pared-down gaming elements – "would have a hoot of a chance in the legislature." This, the editorial stated, was due to the influence of the gaming industry on the legislative process: "All indications are that the racetrack industry controls too many votes to permit a casino expansion that leaves out the tracks."[56]

Indeed, the *Tribune* had reported that between January 2010 and July 2011, the gaming industry had contributed $812,000 to state legislators and other politicians. The biggest donor was Arlington Park racetrack, its owners and related companies at $253,095, accounting for 31 percent of the total. About 72 percent of legislators took money from gaming interests, and those voting for the expansion legislation received an average of nearly 60 percent more from the industry than those voting against it.[57]

One of the top recipients of gaming-industry contributions was also one of the chief sponsors of the expansion legislation. According to the *Tribune*, Rep. Lou Lang, a Democrat from Skokie, had banked $92,000 from gaming interests since the start of 2010, 11 percent of the total. "They give to me because I understand their industry, not because I'm on their side," Lang told the *Tribune*. "What they're looking for is an ear."[58]

We tend to think of the American dream as the ability to navigate our way through society and partake of opportunity in order to achieve success and fulfillment. And often we measure success and fulfillment in material terms.

There is another crucial element of the American dream, however, and it is bound up in the American notion of government of the people, by the people and for the people. Good government and the prudent policies it should create are not meant to inhibit the people nor to deprive them of their freedoms.

Good public policy – including regulation – is meant to protect the people's interests and to clear the pathways of opportunity that lead the people to the American dream. When our leaders in government abandon sound policy for politics and the easy way out, the resulting dysfunction blocks the dream.

The backstories of the Great Recession and the recent quest for gaming expansion in Illinois are parallel narratives of the same phenomenon, one writ large and the other writ smaller. These stories plainly show that today, to a degree that is not only alarming but also harmful, many policy makers believe that they are in business for themselves and that they have been elected and appointed to positions that give them sole proprietorship of the seats they occupy in government.

These stories also show that when political expediency trumps sound public policy – which should be guided by rational planning, cost-benefit analysis and good old-fashioned reasoning – the people lose. Legislators and regulators do not represent the people's interests when they take the easy way out. Instead, they create openings for moneyed interests to step in.

Back in the early 1970s, the only telephone carrier was AT&T. Up until that time, AT&T had not charged for information calls. You would talk to an operator and tell her what number you wanted. She would look it up and give you the number at no charge. But then Illinois Bell decided that it would begin charging for information calls.

I thought it was a terrible idea, so I introduced a bill in the House of Representatives that would not permit Illinois Bell to charge for such calls. The bill came before the public utilities committee, on which I did not serve. After I testified on behalf of my bill, the chairman started to call on people who opposed it. Who appeared to testify in opposition but the chairman of the Illinois Commerce Commission, which regulated telephone rates in the state. I was astounded: Here was a regulator testifying against a consumer bill.

I addressed the committee chairman, saying: "Mr. Chairman, I'm not a member of this committee, and I realize that I cannot question witnesses. But I do have one question that I would like to address to the chairman of the commerce commission."

The committee chairman, being gracious, said, "As long as it won't take a great deal of time, go ahead." I then asked the chairman of the Illinois Commerce Commission: "Does your mother know what you do for a living?" The audience roared. The chairman of the commerce commission gave me a look that could kill a horse, and I lost the bill.

Paying for information calls may seem trivial, but it was a prelude to other industries charging for things that they could do without charging for. When corporations with millions of customers tack on a dollar charge to every bill, those corporations make millions. It's a lot easier to make a million dollars by charging a million people one dollar than to charge one person a million dollars.

Today banks and credit-card companies charge a multitude of fees for things that are part of doing ordinary business, costs that shouldn't be passed on to consumers. But our regulators don't prevent this, because too often they are in the pockets of the industries they regulate.

That's a big problem in America, and it was a significant part of the problem with big banking before the current bust. The regulators were supposed to represent the public interest, but in concert with legislators, they became willing captives of moneyed interests.

As chairman of the Illinois Gaming Board, I have been told by legislators in Springfield that I should be friendlier to the gaming industry. But it's not my job to be their friend; I'm their regulator. I have to be fair and recognize that they're running a business. But at the same time I have to represent and protect the public interest.

The recent economic meltdown has shown the American people the price we pay for accepting the notion that the country works best with the least possible degree of regulation. Even though this has been proven false time and again, we have been told this repeatedly, with no proof and no debate over its veracity. And even though most of us know this is not true, we buy into it anyway.

The ideas we should be buying into are on the agenda of those who have taken to the streets in America: Government should serve the public interest. It should not be the framework for the powerful and the well-connected to enrich themselves at the people's expense.

The bottom line is that the easy way out is not really easy at all. To believe otherwise is to distance ourselves from our American dream.

4
Not So Easy Listening

In 1985, when I became a Cook County Circuit Court judge, a senior judge gave me some advice. He pulled out a little piece of paper and wrote six letters: K Y M S A L. That stood for "Keep your mouth shut and listen." I followed his advice, but he never did.

He was always criticized for interrupting and not listening. Some judges love to scream. I found that those judges who loved to scream had noisy courtrooms; when they screamed, everyone screamed with them.

But if you were soft-spoken and listened, chances were that the lawyers and their clients would listen too. Being in court can be a frightening experience for a litigant or a witness. The judge sits up there in an elevated chair wearing a black robe like an executioner and looks down at people and is supposed to ascertain the truth.

A judge has to listen to all of the parties very carefully in order to get at the truth and to provide a fair and impartial hearing. He has to listen so he can discern the facts as well as the legal theory that is applicable to the case at hand.

He has to listen to learn what axes the parties have to grind and what factors are motivating them. He has to take all of that in and then he has to digest it and roll it around before arriving at a solution.

A judge also has to keep analyzing himself throughout the whole process to make sure that he is not being swayed by one factor or another. Many things can influence perception about a person: personality, way of speaking, appearance and other intangibles.

After I was on the bench for a short time I took a course on listening that was designed for judges. I learned that most people really don't know how to listen to the many different ways that people talk. Some people are bottom-liners: You ask them a question, and they give you a direct answer. Other people are social talkers: They give you more than you asked for because that's the way they think.

My father, Karl, used to say that the only way to learn is to listen, and listen to everyone. People have different experiences, different lifestyles, different motives. Each person speaks differently, even about the same topic. In the film *Rashomon*, four people each recount a different version of the same event.

The atmosphere in a courtroom has to promote justice. This doesn't mean that judges always have to be serious, but they can't be wise guys and they must listen.

These days American political discourse is characterized by a lot of shouting, no shortage of wise guys and a lack of listening – and we're all paying the price. The listening deficit that has permeated our political culture has produced a crisis of confidence that is linked to the unstable economic climate in which we find ourselves.

While factors underlying this instability, including the deregulation of the financial system, have played out over the past several decades from the top down, the listening deficit in our political culture continues to proliferate from the bottom up. Together these two forces are eroding the American dream.

To be sure, our crisis of confidence has been fueled by some critical factors that are beyond the ability of our leaders to fix quickly or to fix at all, whether or not they are listening. Some of these factors are domestic, including prolonged periods of relatively high unemployment; and some are beyond our borders, such as the European debt crisis, which has taken a toll on the U.S. stock market.

But other factors that have shaken our confidence have everything to do with the way our leaders listen – or don't.

In September 2011 Federal Reserve Chairman Ben Bernanke gave a speech in which he linked slow economic growth to American consumers being depressed beyond reason or expectation. Bernanke cited the obvious reasons for consumer wariness, including high unemployment, slow gains in wages, falling real estate values and the high level of U.S. debt.

But economic models based on historic patterns of these factors indicate that consumers should have been spending more. Why weren't they? In effect Bernanke was saying consumers were behaving as if the economy was actually worse than it was.[1] Why was that so?

Perhaps it's because we have a sinking feeling that those whom we have elected to solve our nation's pressing problems just aren't listening, to us or to one another. Instead they're focused primarily on their own narrow partisan politics and the interests of their campaign contributors.

It's a bit like going to the doctor because you feel ill, but she doesn't listen to what you're telling her about what ails you. So you end up feeling even worse than when you sat down on the examining table to explain your symptoms.

Let's consider recent events that are linked to the political listening deficit. On Aug. 5, 2011, the U.S. government's credit rating was downgraded for the first time in American history. Standard & Poor's, the agency that lowered the rating, indicated that the listening deficit in American political culture was a key factor in the agency's decision.

David Beers, global head of sovereign ratings at S&P, told the Associated Press that the agency was concerned "about the degree of uncertainty around the political policy process. The nature of the debate and the difficulty in framing a political consensus ... that was the key consideration," Beers said.[2]

Three days after S&P downgraded the federal government's overall credit rating, it downgraded the credit ratings of Fannie Mae, Freddie Mac and other agencies linked to long-term U.S. debt – and the Dow Jones industrial average closed 634 points lower for the day, losing 5.5 percent; the S&P 500 stock index closed down nearly 6.7 percent.[3]

Indeed, months of political wrangling over the U.S. debt ceiling had ended in an eleventh-hour compromise on July 31, just two days shy of the Treasury Department's estimate of when U.S. borrowing authority would be exhausted. The compromise, which yielded a short-term solution, came after President Obama had walked out of a meeting on the debt ceiling with House Majority Leader Eric Cantor and other congressional leaders on July 13.

This summer brouhaha was preceded in the spring by a round of political drama in which a shutdown of the federal government was averted in April – again at the last minute following months of political sniping. A compromise was finally reached to cut $38.5 billion in federal spending. At the heart of the bickering were hot-button issues including funding for Planned Parenthood and Environmental Protection Agency regulation of greenhouse-gas emissions.[4]

And so, as we find ourselves immersed in a political culture in which listening and compromise have been cast aside, is it any wonder that our confidence has been eroded beyond all reasonable expectations?

Is it any wonder that our crisis of confidence reflects not only the fluctuations of the stock market, the doubts of credit-rating agencies, the hesitancy bordering on unwillingness of employers to invest in the American future by hiring American workers in the present – but also the inability of our leaders to listen to one another and to reach sustainable compromises without continually resorting to brinkmanship?

And is it any wonder that by not listening to one another, in the halls of power and elsewhere, we are witnessing the diminishment of the American dream?

The perils of not listening were illustrated time and again as I presided over cases in divorce court. I had asked to be assigned to divorce court because in the Illinois legislature, I had been the chief sponsor of the Marriage and Dissolution of Marriage Act of 1977.

This law changed the rules of divorce proceedings in Illinois significantly by viewing marriage as a partnership between equals rather than as a financial institution in which the big earner had the most power and therefore the greater rights. I wanted to preside over divorce cases so I could see how well the law was working.

I had one case involving a couple in their 70s who had a substantial estate. The husband had been an immigrant who came to this country and toiled for many years. He sold things from door to door, working from early in the morning to late at night. The wife was quite intelligent and had a keen business sense. She did most of the child rearing herself.

As their children got older, the couple decided to open a food-processing business. She ran the office, and he managed the factory. The business and its eventual offshoots were quite successful, and by means of this success, the couple acquired substantial real estate and investment holdings.

The husband wanted to buy a farm in another state. At first the wife did not agree, but she finally gave in, and they bought the farm. He went off to run the farm, and she remained behind to run their original businesses.

The farm, however, was not a successful enterprise, even though it gave the husband a great deal of satisfaction. The couple had many disagreements about the farm. She wanted to sell it. He loved the farm and didn't want to sell it.

Their differences about the farm became so great that their marriage fell apart, and their case wound up before me in divorce court.

The couple's children were grown, so by this time it was just the two of them fighting over their various and sundry business interests. Looking at it from the outside, the case would have been easy to resolve on its factual merits. The estate was so large that if it were split in half, both the husband and the wife would have had enough money to last three lifetimes.

Emotions were running high, though – so much so that the level of hostility between the parties had started to interfere with the normal functioning of their businesses. For example, both the husband and wife needed to sign checks, but when one party signed, the other party would refuse. So I appointed a receiver to assist with the running of the businesses.

Consulting with both parties' lawyers, the receiver said it appeared to him that the case should be settled on the basis of a 50-50 split because that was the way the businesses had been set up. He also said that given the couple's age, there were no factors such as child support that would logically lead to any other division of assets. It was clear-cut.

The wife, however, believed that she was entitled to 90 percent of the estate, and her lawyer convinced her that she was within her rights to make such a demand. He told her that if the case were tried, she would get her 90 percent. Emotions were running so high that the parties couldn't reach a settlement. So the case went to trial over a period of several months, and both the husband and the wife spent a lot of money on legal fees.

During the final arguments, the wife's lawyer got up and said: "She was a wonderful wife. She raised the children, she provided a wonderful home. She was a great businesswoman and did everything that a wife should do. She was just magnificent."

Then the husband jumped up out of control and shouted: "You think she's so wonderful, you think she's so marvelous? We'll be divorced in a couple of weeks – and then you can marry her!"

In the end I ruled on the facts in the way that logic dictated – a 50-50 split. The object lesson of the case is this: As a party to a disagreement, if you come in with an open mind and let the facts prevail, the issue should be relatively easy to settle. But if you don't listen and let emotions get the better of you, you're likely to make a costly mistake. When emotion sets in, it deadens the sense of rationality.

About 90 percent of civil cases that reach the courtroom should be settled, not tried. I made an effort to settle all types of cases that came before me, because in the law a settlement eliminates a lot of things that the parties shouldn't necessarily have to expend, including money, emotional energy and time. It is much better to conserve these precious resources by reaching a settlement.

This almost always requires a compromise in which needs of both parties are met. Each party makes concessions, but nobody surrenders. To reach that compromise, the parties have to listen.

But you can't settle if you don't listen and reason logically. This principle is every bit as applicable in the legislative chamber as it is in the courtroom.

A great problem in America these days, however, is that more people are talking politics but fewer people are listening. There appear to be many reasons for this listening deficit.

The first is technology, or what could be called the gadetization of our culture. Technology is wonderful, but it can also have drawbacks. Take cellphones. If you watch how folks use their phones, you will see people texting and tweeting, taking pictures and hopping on the Internet to get directions.

Despite all of its advantages, this kind of technology affects people's ability to listen by fragmenting the process of communication into many virtual realms where you can leave your ears behind.

The second reason that listening has been set back is the emergence of the culture of instant gratification, a 24 hour-a-day phenomenon driven by the mentality of "I want it all, and I want it now." This doesn't bode well for the art of listening, which usually takes time and patience when done effectively.

A third reason for our listening gap is the predominance of visual imagery in popular culture, which is also linked to advances in technology. The movies that draw the biggest audiences these days are those that depict speed, car chases, monsters exploding. It's action, action, action.

Contrast this with films of earlier eras and live theater, which focus on words and ideas that we understand by listening. But as we watch computer-generated cities crumble and oceans overspill their shorelines, we don't have to actively engage in listening and thinking. Instead we just sit back and become passive observers.

But perhaps the reason for the listening deficit that is tied most directly to our political culture is the gradual transformation of the broadcast news media, in particular (but not limited to) the 24/7 variety. News talk shows are supposed to provide analysis, but many of the more popular ones have become platforms for four or five talking heads to take a stab at discussing the various issues of the day.

By and large, however, these talking heads have more celebrity than intellect, more star power than brain power. They appear to be listening to one another, but they're really there as easily identifiable types: liberal, conservative; Republican, Democrat.

In effect, these so-called news shows are contests among commentators who in their own minds represent certain groups. They attack one another, and the public is encouraged to take sides. Who are you with, Fox News or MSNBC? The 24/7 networks have a lot of time to fill, and rather than give us depth and substance, they give us the fight of the week. There's a lot of heat but little light.

This plays directly into the listening deficit in our political culture. The shouting is a diversion from the real issues, and it doesn't offer the fodder that we need to consider in order to be able to solve our problems. The public becomes so overwhelmed by the drama that we start to believe that the drama is the substance.

But we can't substitute drama for reason in order to solve our problems. When we substitute drama for reason, the result is that we don't understand what we're hearing.

For example, people say they're against unions because they're ruining the economy. The fact is that the American dream became reality for more people when unions were stronger.

Unionized factory workers became able to buy summer homes, where they could go on vacation and relax. Before the rise of unions, fewer people had cars. As unions grew stronger, the automobile became a staple of the emerging middle class. Now unions are being battered by public opinion, by many of the very same people whom unions could help.

On many such issues we are headed in a direction that's contrary to what's good for us. People scream about paying teachers a decent salary in an age when our children need a good education more than ever. People will cheer on athletes who earn multimillion-dollar salaries at the same time that the cheerleaders need at least two people in each of their families to work to make ends meet.

Many people say they are scared to death about socialism, given the U.S. government bailouts of various industries in recent years. When most Americans hear the word "socialism," their minds are instantly set against it.

A fact not making its way into the conversation, though, is that during the Great Depression, FDR turned to socialist measures to keep American capitalism alive. Socialism is not a perfect system, of course. But to solve problems, we have to consider all sorts of options.

We live by catchwords, sound bites and labels. When we use labels, we don't have to listen. When we don't listen, we can't talk to one another to reach the solutions we need. We burn up a lot of precious resources in the process – just like that older divorcing couple who passed the point of listening to each other by the time they reached my courtroom.

Unlike them, however, as a society we can hardly afford such expenditures in this day and age.

If you tell a liberal that someone is a conservative, the liberal attacks. If you tell a conservative that someone's a liberal, the conservative attacks. Everyone wants to be seen as moderate, but no one knows what that is.

The act of political labeling has become the debate in and of itself, and when that happens, we no longer look at the substance of the issues that confront us. Take the word "terrorist." Immediately after 9/11, President Bush stood America on its head by labeling everyone who didn't agree with our policies as being a threat when he declared that "either you are with us, or you are with the terrorists."

There is no question that we must be diligent and defend ourselves against all real threats, and we must take steps to prevent those threats that we reasonably can. But we have to be able to discern what the real threats are.

We must do this so that we can avoid at all costs sending our young men and women to die on foreign soil in the course of chasing a terrorist threat that is not real, as we did in Iraq. When we put our young people at risk by using a false premise to gain political or economic advantage, we are guilty of the worst of all possible sins.

The Bush administration came up with the idea of issuing threat warnings by color: yellow, orange, red. We heard announcements through the media that today is an orange day, a yellow day, a purple day. No one knew what that meant, but the concept was being instilled in us that we were under threat all the time. We were made to think that we were in danger every minute of every day – just a different-colored threat on any given day.

When that is hammered into people's heads, they believe that they're constantly in harm's way. This makes them more willing to do things they wouldn't ordinarily do and think in ways they wouldn't normally think if they could look at the matter calmly and logically.

If you sit someone down in a chair and hit him in the face every five minutes, he's going to expect to be hit five minutes from now. When people are trained to react a certain way, they do not need to think or to listen. They respond like Pavlov's dogs did to ringing bells.

One of the big ideas that we have been hit in the face with repeatedly in recent years is that when big companies get bigger and face financial jeopardy, the government must bail them out because they are too big to fail. The people can grumble about executives' salaries, but the government must underwrite the big banks and the big investment houses because they're too big to fail, or so we are told.

Executive salaries are too high, it's true. That should be addressed. But the fact is that those high salaries wouldn't be an issue if the financial industry didn't have a free hand. No one wants to rein it in.

The banks, investment houses and insurance companies are immense, and they have immense power. The people who run them have immense power. We can't touch them because we don't ever get that far in the discussion. Instead we are satisfied with complaining about their salaries.

If the financial industry were regulated as closely as it was prior to the Reagan era, those salaries would not be what they are. That's the discussion we should be having in the first place. But we aren't, and as a result, a lot of people got hurt in the Great Recession, and many have yet to recover.

The idea that democracy depends on an enlightened electorate has been part of American political culture since the time of Benjamin Franklin and Thomas Jefferson. It's not that the public has to start taking courses in every issue of national import. But we should be knowledgeable about the nuts and bolts of the issues rather than rely on emotional arguments – and at least part of that knowledge should come from public discourse and debate.

If we are not enlightened about the issues confronting us and we don't listen to one another, then we are not going to be able to debate the issues intelligently or to solve the underlying problems.

What does that scenario bode for the American dream?

Perhaps the most dangerous factor of all the factors contributing to our hobbled listening culture is that today we are in a climate of hyperpartisan politics, which is built on the illusion of power.

When I was in the state legislature, Republicans and Democrats spoke to one another. We tried to listen to one another. This wasn't true for everyone, but it was true for most of us. When I was chair of the House judiciary committee, I needed and wanted the cooperation of the minority party, which was the Republican Party.

The minority spokesman and I were diametrically opposed on most issues. I would always know what bills he wanted called, and he knew mine. He also knew that I was going to give his party a fair hearing and allow its members to call as many witnesses as they wanted. And I knew that if he were the chairman, he would have done the same for my party. We would have long debates on the floor of the House, and sometimes our sessions would last into the wee hours of the morning.

Some years before, in the early 1970s, I had introduced the first bill on no-fault divorce in Illinois. I told my fellow judiciary committee members that I thought the issue should be debated on the floor of the House because more and more states were adopting no-fault divorce. I was sure that the bill would be defeated, but I wanted to get the issue on the public agenda.

At that time Republicans controlled the House, but the chairman allowed me to go forward. My bill went down on the floor, as I knew it would. But the issue became part of public discourse, and this was important because many complex, sensitive issues are not solved quickly. They have to be debated, they have to be studied. They have to be ripe for the public to engage.

As it turned out, it took more than a decade of public debate before no-fault divorce became law in Illinois in 1984. That debate and the public awareness it generated were the keys to effecting positive change. If we don't have that debate, that exchange, that listening, then all we have are angry voices. And today in America we have a lot of angry voices.

The amount of discussion on the floor of the House of Representatives in Illinois is really quite limited these days. The primary reason for this change is that the party in control won't listen to the other party.

This very same phenomenon was painfully apparent on the national level during the first two years of the Obama administration. With the Democrats controlling not only the White House but also Congress, the political gridlock that materialized was remarkable, to say the least.

In February 2010 *The New York Times* characterized Exhibit A of the gridlock as "the unwillingness of the two parties to compromise to control a national debt that is rising to dangerous heights. ... Rarely has the political system seemed more polarized and less able to solve big problems that involve trust, tough choices and little short-term gain.

"The main urgency for both parties," the *Times* observed, "seems to be about pinning blame on the other, before November's elections, for deficits now averaging $1 trillion a year, the largest since World War II relative to the size of the economy."[5]

In my 14 years in the legislature, I learned that part of insider fighting is being able to listen to the other side. You have to understand that you can't always get your full legislative package, and that sometimes you have to move more slowly than you want while still keeping the big picture in mind.

You have to keep pushing to get your issues on the public agenda while still listening to other people. You never go to anyone for a vote when it is diametrically opposed to what he believes in or what her constituents want. You can disagree with your opponents, but you have to respect them.

In the legislature I found that I could talk to people, and we could compare our ideas. I knew in my mind that I wasn't necessarily right, and they knew in their minds that they weren't necessarily right. And we knew that in all probability, no one was absolutely right, and the correct path lay somewhere in the middle. It was only by having a public discussion and exchanging ideas that we made progress.

When the legislature was in session, I would make the 200-mile drive to Springfield with three representatives from Chicago. We were two Democrats and two Republicans and we rode together for years. We would debate the issues going down, we would debate coming back and we would debate on the floor of the House. But we were friends. There was no animosity or hatred. We respected one another's opinions.

When I began as a freshman legislator, the old pros on both sides of the aisle told me the same thing that veteran judge did before I took my place on the bench: Keep your mouth shut and listen. But as a young legislator, I didn't heed this advice, and I started introducing bills that I thought should be on the public agenda, such as no-fault divorce.

Another thing I did early on was to get to know all of my colleagues in the legislature, regardless of their party or where in the state they hailed from. I made it my business to listen to their points of view. There's an age-old truism in Illinois politics that Chicagoans and downstaters don't mix. But in the process of meeting the other 176 representatives who were in the Illinois House at the time, I came to admire and appreciate reps from downstate like Kenny Boyle.

Kenny was a Democrat from Macoupin County, southwest of Springfield. He was heavyset, and in the summertime he would wear white suits like a southern farmer, with suspenders and the whole bit. Kenny would talk like a hick who just fell off the truck, but he had graduated at the top of his law school class at the University of Illinois. He was a brilliant guy, but he loved that small-town façade.

In the 1970s the Chicago Bar Association was dominated by corporate lawyers. A group of them came to Springfield to lobby for a bill that would have given more control to majority stockholders at the expense of small investors. The Chicago lawyers presented their bill looking very smug in their beautiful silk suits and stockings.

Kenny was sitting there in his shirt sleeves and suspenders and said: "Gentlemen, I know that you're big lawyers from the city of Chicago, and I'm just a poor country lawyer. We don't have those big co-operations [he was punning on 'corporations'] down in Macoupin County. All we have is poor farm folk.

"When I get a fee for my services, sometimes I get a few chickens, sometimes I get some eggs, and if I handle a big case, I might get a side of beef."

The Chicago lawyers were smirking at Kenny, but he continued: "Please pardon my ignorance, 'cause I don't know too much about these things. Would you mind if I ask you a few questions?" And they smiled in their condescending way and told him to go ahead.

By the time Kenny asked his sixth question, he had destroyed the lawyers by showing how terrible their bill was. A seemingly unlikely challenger to their highfalutin manners and ideas, Kenny Boyle had compelled them to listen. And those fancy lawyers went back to Chicago not knowing what hit them.

The same kind of arrogance that precludes listening to the other side in the political arena also played out in my courtroom on many an occasion.

The stakes in a divorce case, of course, are of a different magnitude from what's at stake in the inability of our government to agree on a formula for getting the national debt under control. The result, however, is the same: When the parties won't listen and refuse to reach a compromise, everyone stands to lose.

I presided over a divorce case that centered on custody of the couple's three minor children. The wife had been an alcoholic and had reached the point where she decided to go into treatment for her condition. She told her husband that she intended to do this, and she asked for his help and support.

The husband was a rather cold-blooded guy, and he turned his wife down. He didn't agree that she should go into treatment, and he wasn't going to be supportive of her. At this point in their marriage he felt that he was done with the whole situation. He was also very calculating, figuring that his wife had proven herself to be so incompetent that no court would ever give her custody of the children.

Simply put, he believed that he was so powerful in the relationship that he did not *have* to listen. He believed that the children were his – so much so that he had already turned the oldest child, who was no longer a minor, against the mother to the point that they had no relationship. The three younger children were still somewhat attached to her but more so to him.

The wife went into treatment and did what people in treatment for alcoholism often do: She turned to religion as part of her recovery process. She then returned to work, worked steadily and succeeded in keeping off the bottle. Still, she and her husband decided to divorce, and in court the husband petitioned for custody of the three minor children.

The psychiatric reports on both parties indicated that the husband should get custody of the children because the wife was somewhat childlike in her approach to life. Even so, these experts indicated that she was doing well because of her newfound faith and other factors, and it appeared unlikely that she would relapse into alcoholism.

After reading the reports, I told the parties that I was dismayed by the husband's inability to understand his wife's position. I told them that I thought I should not decide the case until they went through counseling and therapy together.

I told the husband that I expected him to attend these sessions and apply himself, because I felt that while the wife had her failings, the children needed their mother as they were growing up. I stressed that the most important thing was for the children to have the support of both parents, not just the one parent who had alienated the kids from the other parent.

I continued the case for six months while the husband and wife were supposed to go to therapy. After that time I received reports from the therapist and the other psychiatrists involved saying that the husband did not attend most of the sessions because he thought that there was no way that his wife was ever going to be able to get custody of the children.

When the couple returned to court, the husband appeared confident, and the wife appeared fearful of losing her children. I told the parties that I was fully aware of what the earlier reports had said, indicating that custody should go to the husband. But in light of recent developments, I told them that I wasn't going to make a decision just yet.

I could have taken the easy way out and ruled according to the original reports, all three of which favored custody for the father. But I didn't, because being a judge isn't an easy job. The future of those children was in my hands. And if I took the easy way out, I could have done those kids some real damage.

I turned to the husband and said: "You think that you have everything going your way. But I must tell you, I am coming to the conclusion that while your wife may be unfit to handle the children, you may be an unfit father because you're not doing what's in their best interest.

"So," I told him, "I'm continuing the matter for another six months. I'm ordering you into therapy again, and if you do not go into therapy with an open mind and with the attitude of cooperating with the therapist and your wife – for the sake of your children – then you may not get custody. The truth of the matter is that I may not give the children to either one of you, and I may place them in some other custodial care."

I could tell that the husband was upset, because he was now facing a situation that he hadn't thought possible – that he wouldn't get custody of his children.

After another six months, the couple came back to court. This time the husband had complied with the therapy, and he seemed to understand that his soon-to-be ex-wife had to be a part of their children's lives. He was cooperating with the therapist and working with the children.

The wife was in a much better place, and while the children were not totally happy – they wanted their parents to stay together – they were happier than before. They were seeing their mother, and even the oldest child had now reconciled with her.

So I granted custody of the children to the husband and gave the wife liberal visitation privileges. As the case concluded, the family was happier, although not whole. The kids were happier, the mother was happier and the father finally got the picture that this was how it should be.

The object lesson, of course, is that when we don't listen, we stand to lose more than we ever thought possible. If the husband hadn't started to listen, he would have lost his children and been devastated. Someone had to put the brakes on his arrogance for the sake of the children. He thought he was in such a powerful position that he couldn't lose.

But the fact of the matter is that we never have complete power, because power is nothing more than an illusion.

People and institutions don't get power by themselves; they get it when others believe they are powerful. But that belief can change quickly, and power can wane just as quickly.

This was evident when S&P downgraded the credit rating of the U.S. government. The agency was in effect telling Washington: Because you can't get your act together, you're no longer as powerful as we once thought you were.

And because you're no longer as powerful as we thought you were when we gave you that AAA rating, now we're downgrading you to AA+.

The worst kind of not listening is the kind where someone makes up his or her mind in advance and deliberately chooses to disregard the facts and the rules of the game. When this happens in the law and in politics, self-interest trumps the public interest every time.

I spent more than half my tenure as a judge presiding in chancery court, where one type of case I handled was appeals on rulings by municipal, county and state agencies concerning reinstatement of various types of licenses. These can include driver's licenses, licenses to practice certain professions, liquor licenses. People come to chancery court to appeal denials by administrative hearing officers on reinstatement of licenses.

I handled many appeals dealing with driver's licenses, especially in cases where the license had been revoked because of drunken driving. When a license is revoked for DUI, the driver must go through counseling and take several other steps to get it back.

I would often get cases in which people had gone through counseling. They also had statements from health professionals that they were recovering and had no current alcohol problems, and they had affidavits of support from their employers. In any given case, I would receive the same file of these documents that the administrative hearing officer had seen, and I had to determine whether the officer had ruled correctly.

Often I would be astounded by the fact that here was an individual who had taken all of the necessary steps to get his license reinstated, sometimes months or even years ago, who had a record that basically said: This person is fine to get his driver's license back.

I would find letters from the employer indicating that the appellant had worked for the company for a number of years and was a valued employee; that there had been only one DUI incident; and that he had a job waiting for him. The record also showed that the appellant needed to drive in order to reach his place of employment because he lived far away and there was no public transportation available.

In such cases I would sometimes also see evidence that the driver's wife, who was also working, had to get up early in the morning to take her husband to work and then return home to get the kids off to school before going to her own job. So it appeared to be an extreme hardship for the person making the appeal not to be able to drive.

Over time I came to believe that in clear-cut cases such as these, administrative hearing officers had not reinstated the licenses out of fear that there was a chance the drivers might get involved in other DUI incidents, perhaps even accidents in which someone might get injured or worse. If a license was reinstated and such an event occurred, then this would reflect poorly on the hearing officer's judgment as well as on the reputation of the agency as a whole.

I overruled administrative hearing officers in dozens of such cases because it was clear that they had not properly considered the factual evidence in their decisions not to reinstate licenses. It was, in essence, a matter of listening, but the officers had not given the drivers and their evidence a fair hearing.

It appeared that the officers' thinking was: Give it to the judge to do, and if the driver relapses, then the consequences will be on the judge's head. Then the agency could say: We wouldn't give this guy his driver's license back, but the judge did – and look what a terrible mistake he made.

The hearing officers were hedging their bets against the system to avoid the possibility of taking a hit. Fortunately, I never took a hit in my rulings on these cases. But if a ruling would have come back to bite me, it would have come back to bite me. That was my job.

This pattern repeated itself not only with driver's licenses but with other types of licenses as well. I had a case that involved an elderly optometrist in his 80s. He had fallen ill and for a short period of time had failed to take the necessary courses to keep his professional certifications up to date. After he recovered he did all of the things that were required to get his license back. But surprisingly the state Division of Professional Regulation didn't reinstate it.

When I got the case file, I saw that the optometrist had never been accused of professional wrongdoing. The only reason for the denial that I could infer was that the agency presumed that he might not be competent because of his age. But there was no evidence of that, so I reinstated his license.

This was another case of an agency not listening to the evidence and not following its own rules. Judgments were being made on the basis of self-interest by those who were passing the buck, protecting their own hides and looking for a fall guy.

Looking for a fall guy has become part of American political culture. People love to complain, but they don't want to make decisions. They wait for someone else to act. The political debate in the two years leading up to the 2010 midterm elections was a case in point.

On one side, the party that was not in power engaged in name-calling about the party that was in power. These names bore no semblance to reality, such as calling the president a socialist, and some on the fringes even insisting that he wasn't born in the United States.

More than that, the minority party closed its mind to any programs that were forthcoming from the majority party and voted them down, one after the other, as a deliberate tactical maneuver to try to stymie the opposition.

On the other side, the party that was in power functioned much like the hearing officers whose decisions I overruled in chancery court. This party was fearful of giving the American public effective solutions to policy problems for fear of taking a hit, so they passed the buck for their own inaction on to the naysayers.

The party in power passed health care and financial reforms that were tepid at best, and then they turned around and said: "We couldn't do any better because the naysayers are stopping us."

Many Americans, I found, were all too happy to make excuses for the party in power. I heard many say, "Well, look at Congress." To which I said, "Yes, look at Congress."

The president was elected with a substantial majority in both houses but was unable or unwilling to get legislation with real teeth passed. Some would say: "Yes, he had a big majority, but ... look at the Blue Dog Democrats. They're not going along with what the party wants."

Well, what about the Blue Dogs? It's the president who has the bully pulpit. He can go on TV anytime he wants to espouse his programs. When it came to health care, the president said: "Let Congress do it, because I don't want to make the same mistake that Bill Clinton made." But that was a very poor excuse.

When it came to reining in the financial institutions that have put this country in grave danger, what we got from the president and his majority party were a lot of platitudes and legislation that lacked real teeth. But these are not sufficient to serve and protect the public interest.

All the while, some of the most prominent media outlets were staging shout fests instead of listening to what the people were saying. Celebrity talking heads don't report the news – they want to *be* the news. They command a share of attention that is out of all reasonable proportion to what is being reported about the substance of the issues that we are facing.

More than four years after the Great Recession began, people are still losing their homes. The national unemployment rate still hovers above 8 percent. The cost of higher education has gone through the roof.

You can't achieve the American dream if you're hungry, if you don't have a place to live, if you don't have job, if higher education is inaccessible. Food, housing, employment and education are the things upon which the American dream is built.

The listening deficit in our political culture exacts a great price on the dream. The deficit prevents the government from enacting policies that enable the people to make their way and have a fair shot at making the dream come true.

The government cannot provide the people with everything, but neither should it sanction the privileged and powerful to run away with the majority of the wealth. The system should provide a mechanism for balance, and that balance should benefit the greater good.

But we are in the grips of a system failure that is sucking the greater good into the void. The Democrats tell us: Don't re-elect the Republicans, because theirs is a failed philosophy that has proved time and again to be the wrong way to go. And the Democrats are correct.

The Republicans tell us: The Democrats don't know how to govern. And in this regard, the Republicans are also correct. In passing the buck for their inaction on to the naysayers, the Democrats don't really want to take a stand. They want to play it safe.

But we can't afford to play it safe in these times.

Today many people have the sense that the problems we face are so overwhelming that finding solutions is all but impossible. The situation is too complicated to fix, people say. Passing legislation is too difficult. Too many people disagree about too many things.

But nothing is that difficult. Anything that the human mind puts together, the human mind should be able to understand. When people sit and reason together, they can come up with viable solutions.

The most complex case that I had as a judge was an insurance case. A battery manufacturer that had dozens of factories all over the country had been putting toxic chemicals into the soil for decades, and a multitude of insurance companies had insured these factories over time. So the case boiled down to determining how much of the toxic damage each particular insurance company was responsible for covering during specific time periods.

When I initially called the case, nearly everyone in the courtroom stood up and approached the bench because there were dozens of lawyers representing all those insurance companies.

The case, which had been assigned to me on a random basis, was so complex that many observers said: We'll come back in 20 years and see where you are on it. My fellow judges smiled and expressed relief that they hadn't gotten stuck with it.

It was up to me to find a way forward. The lawyers for the insurance companies knew from the outset that this would be a gargantuan task. It was difficult, but we came up with a plan to lay out all of the individual damage claims to see which issues were predominant in each one.

Initially I had committees of plaintiffs and defendants sit together to define the predominant issues, and then we selected the claims that were based on these issues. My thinking was to get the parties to listen to one another and define the basic issues at the outset in order to facilitate the proceedings.

Sorting through the claims to identify the predominant issues was a complex process. The issues included how to define a time period; how to reach conclusions about how long the insurance coverage was applicable; how to define which company would pay for what toxic damage.

We narrowed it down to the three locations in which the claims were most representative of these issues. We decided to try these three claims at one time, and then the case would be sent up for appeal. When it came back, we would use the ruling of the state appellate court and my ruling to see how far we could get in settling the remaining claims.

That's how it played out, and it became a precedent-setting case in insurance law. We had been confronted with issues that had no precedent because the sheer number of variables made the process so cumbersome and difficult. There were all sorts of legal theories that had not been tested. We had to find a formula that everyone could live with.

This long and complex process took several years. But we worked through it much faster than anyone had anticipated because the lawyers were willing to cooperate in order to define the issues. In other words, they listened to one another.

It wasn't an emotional case. The challenge was plain: How were we going to figure things out? It was a matter of rolling up our sleeves and doing what we had to do to get through it.

When you throw up your hands and say that a problem is too difficult, you've already said you're not going to deal with it. But we can't afford to throw up our hands and walk away from the issues confronting us. It's like the hole in the ozone layer: The bigger it gets, the more destructive the effects of climate change become.

Take the recent financial crisis. People say that the financial industry is so complex that we can't understand it. But we can understand the financial crisis by examining the financial system as it is, which is complex by design.

For example, equity companies concoct corporate structures that are mind-boggling. One branch of the corporation has all of the voting stock; another branch holds all of the debt. They're actually separate corporations that are bound together.

The equity companies' end game is to maneuver within legal limits to gain advantages including lower tax liabilities and beefed-up balance sheets in order to attract investors.

Understanding who does what gets to be so complex that many throw up their hands and say the matter is too difficult to understand. However, regulators have to work hard to understand the system in order to solve its problems. The financial industry, like all industries, can be regulated properly only if all of its parts are understood.

The same kind of complexity by design was evident in the recent health care reform bill. At 2,000 pages long, it bore the distinct imprint of lobbyists.

The more complex the bill, the more language it has. The more language it has, the greater the chance for conflicting statements. When there are conflicting statements, those with vested interests can play one off the other to accomplish opposing goals. The result is a watered-down piece of legislation that ends up benefiting the moneyed interests more than the people.

The way to make sense of the complexity is to ask questions and then listen to the answers. You have to understand what you're arguing about before you can come to a conclusion. Today many of the arguments that we hear on the 24/7 cable networks are inept because they're based on arguing rather than on understanding the issues. People find it a lot easier to argue without knowing the facts. But we can't just create our own reality; we have to understand reality as it is.

Apparently, some are ready to believe that it will take nothing less than divine intervention to get us to listen to one another so we can find our way through these perplexing times. On the Sunday in late August 2011 that Hurricane Irene slammed into New England, Republican congresswoman and presidential contender Michele Bachmann said the great storm was a sign from God to get politicians to listen to the American people.

"I don't know how much God has to do to get the attention of politicians," Bachmann said during a Florida campaign swing that day. "We've had an earthquake; we've had a hurricane. He said, 'Are you going to start listening to me here?' Listen to the American people because the American people are roaring right now. They know government is on a morbid obesity diet, and we've got to rein in the spending."[6]

Bachmann's linking Hurricane Irene to divine intervention stirred up a media storm, which led her to backtrack quickly and say that she had made the statement in jest. But the predicament of our not-so-easy listening culture is no joke, and it boils down to this: On the one hand, the problems we face today are complex. But on the other hand, they not as insoluble as we think they are.

A main reason – if not the main reason – that we think our problems are so difficult to solve is that we have stopped listening to one another. However, at some point the difficulty of our problems and the degree of our listening deficit are linked: The bigger the deficit becomes, the harder it is to solve the problems.

And the longer we fail to listen and our problems go unsolved, the more we imperil our American dream.

5
Goodbye, American Dream?

I had coffee recently with a friend who is also in his 80s. He went on and on about the situation the country is in. He said that when he talks to people, he finds a general feeling of desperation out there: "If you talk to them about what's wrong and what the country needs, they say, 'What difference does it make? The president can't do anything about this, no one can. It's too complicated, it's too tough.'"

My friend went on to say he has the feeling that most people who are up in years think: "Thank goodness I don't have to start all over again, but I worry about my grandchildren. What are they going to do?"

I thought about what he said, and it occurred to me that civilizations don't last forever. And this reminded me of the story of the Tower of Babel.

The Book of Genesis tells us that generations after the Great Flood, a united humanity spoke a single language. They came to a great plain in Babylon, where they decided to build a tower with its top in the heavens to project their sense of power and self-importance. Instead of using stone, a natural material, they constructed the tower from brick and mortar, which they made themselves.

There are different interpretations of why what happened next happened. But the story goes that God saw the tower and said something like: "The people [are] one, and they all have one language; and this [building of the tower] they begin to do; and now nothing will be restrained from them, which they have imagined to do."[1]

So perhaps to put a damper on their grandiose and self-important endeavor, God decided to confound the people's language. From then on, the people could not understand one another because they spoke a multitude of languages, and they had to stop building their tower.

I believe that today we are playing out our own Tower of Babel story. We have lost our common language, despite the fact that technology has given us modes of communication that we could not have dreamed of a mere 25 years ago. We have allowed the people who aspire to build their towers to the heavens – the people of moneyed interests and those of our elected leaders who have been co-opted – to confound our common language and to Babelize our society.

More often than not these days, in realms of public policy we talk at cross purposes and fail to find consensus until it is too late, after the damage of not listening, not compromising and resorting to brinkmanship has already been done. It's no wonder, then, that the word "babble" is so often associated with the Tower of Babel tale.

But because I am not given to interpreting current events on the basis of Scripture, I don't believe that our modern-day Tower of Babel predicament comes from above. Rather, it is entirely of our own making.

We must find the way to take our power back and find the way back to a common language so that we can continue to build our tower, which is really the good life in an open and free society where all people have the opportunities and tools to prosper. In other words, we need to find our way back to the American dream.

To do that, we have to step back and take a hard look at our collective American self, starting with our political process and the policies that emerge from it. We have to take a hard look at what we want and at what divides us. It sounds easy, but it's not – because looking at ourselves honestly and critically is a tough task.

In 2008 and 2010 we had two national elections, both of which produced changes in leadership, reversals in the status quo. But these changes have been superficial, and that's the problem. In effecting flip-flops in the parties that control the White House and Congress, we think that we have achieved great change. We have convinced ourselves – wrongly so – that the appearance of change is in fact the real thing, change itself.

We're still suffering many of the effects of a deep recession, and the big banks and investment houses still control the direction of much of the economy. It seems that the flip-flops in these two elections signaled that the people stood up and said: "We don't want this." But despite changing the parties that lead at the top levels of government, the situation has remained unchanged, and real change may still very well elude us.

All you have to do is talk to people to understand that most Americans support the idea of a health care system that would ensure basic coverage for all people. They support regulation of the financial markets. They want education for all of our children and higher education to be accessible at a reasonable cost.

Then the Tea Party rises and seems to speak a different language. Tea Partiers say: "We want to get the government off our backs." But they also seem to be saying that they want the rights that are promised to us all in the Constitution according to the principles set out in the Declaration of Independence. They want a government by the people and for the people. They want the right to life, liberty and the pursuit of happiness – which together give us the formula for the American dream.

The Tea Party's main demand for less government is based on cutting taxes and social spending. But the Tea Party does not address two major areas in which government is very much in our lives on a constant, daily basis – albeit in ways that are not immediately perceptible.

The first is the great degree to which the financial markets have been deregulated. This is not the result of a naturally occurring, free-market process. It is, rather, the result of deliberate political decisions to *de*-regulate the market. These decisions have been made over the last 30 years at the highest levels of government by people who have deep and abiding connections to the financial industry.

The resulting government deregulation of the markets – which has been carried out and successively amplified by Democratic and Republican presidents and Congresses alike – has not benefited most of the people, as we have seen in recent years. It has served to enrich only a very few to a degree beyond ordinary imagination. This lack of regulation has had the effect of further stratifying American society by class, polarizing the rich and the poor to a greater degree and shrinking the middle class in between. The net result is that fewer and fewer of us have access to the American dream.

The second area of immense government presence is military spending. While some Tea Party leaders have said there are no sacred cows when it comes to chopping the federal budget, including military spending,[2] the party has yet to focus on the magnitude of military spending and the cost of our military presence in dozens of countries around the world.

The outlay of so much of our national treasure to project American military power, which results in less of the pie being available to us for health care, education and other social spending, is not a perceptible target for the movement whose purpose is to scale back the scope of the federal government.

And so we have created our own Tower of Babel, speaking in different tongues and not understanding one another. There's a great disconnect between what people say they want, what they really want and how they say we can get it.

The greater the confusion of this babble, the easier it becomes to avoid making decisions. We either throw up our hands in despair or hitch a ride with false prophets.

In 2008 we were hungry for change, so we threw the bums out. Then the 24/7 newspeople observed: "Things have changed. It's a move to the left." In 2010 we still wanted change, so we threw the bums out again. Then the 24/7 people told us: "This is a real change; it's a turn toward the right." After both elections we were told: "The people have spoken. This is clear from the election results."

But I would submit that no such thing is clear, and that the 24/7 people have been dead wrong. The meaning of those election results is this: Nothing has really changed, because neither of the two major political parties, as they are now constituted, will satisfy the needs of the people.

There is great risk, even danger, in believing that we have achieved change when all we really have achieved is the appearance of change. We have recently found ourselves on the brink of economic disaster, and we may face such a disaster if we don't stop being satisfied with the mere appearance of change. We need to find our way back to effecting real change, and it's about time the people wake up and understand that.

You cannot have a society where the financial markets are deregulated, where people cannot afford health care, where young people cannot afford to continue their education without starting their working lives mired in debt. I would say that we can't continue to fiddle while Rome burns, but that's not a strong enough metaphor.

If we find ourselves in another Great Depression, our entire way of life will crumble. This may sound alarmist, and there's not much public talk about it. But given the state of our nation and economy, we should be asking ourselves: What happens if we have another such depression? It's not out of the realm of possibility.

We have to give serious consideration to how bad things could really get. We have to educate ourselves on the issues. We have to take a longer view and demand new policies on a range of issues including interest rates, energy prices and campaign-finance reform.

We are frightened by what we see happening. People have lost their jobs, their houses and their pensions – or are having a much harder time holding on to them. We know things are bad, and we're afraid they can get worse. But we want to believe that they won't. It's human nature to shy away from our fears. But we're not going to change anything until we face them.

Before we can return to optimism, we have to be willing to look at ourselves, at our politicians and at our public policies objectively and critically. We have to look in the mirror and see things as they are, not as we want them to be. Seeing things as they are is the prerequisite for getting to where we want to go.

When we do that, it's natural to be pessimistic in the short term, because things have gotten worse in recent years. Things will turn around only if we dig in and really start fighting for change, because the Great Recession has proved that many old truisms aren't true anymore.

For example, we have been led to believe that there are few better investments than real estate because its value only appreciates. But the bottom has fallen out of the real estate market, and it could tumble further still.

We have been sold the idea that home ownership should be accessible to as many Americans as possible, even at the cost of making mortgages available to buyers who could not afford to make down payments and then allowing the trading of risky mortgage-based derivatives in a deregulated market, with disastrous results.

We also have been hypnotized by the mantras that the way America creates greatness is to let the financial markets run free, and happiness will come our way because any one of us can reach the top. Americans have long lived under the delusion that capitalism is a wonderful system because it gives us the *possibility* that each and every one of us can make it to the top and become super-rich. But the *probability* is that only a small number of people will make it to the top.

The idea that it's possible for any of us to become super-rich has been imbued in the American mentality so thoroughly that we have come to believe that anything that's good for rich people is good for us all – because someday any of us could become rich ourselves. This ultimately leads us to vote against our own interests when we agree to policies that benefit mostly those at the very top.

In the process we're trading our democracy for oligarchy, in which a few powerful groups at the top of society reap a disproportionate share of the wealth and block opportunity for the majority. We are becoming slaves to other people's greed while deluding ourselves that we'll be in their company someday.

We need to get back to the idea that fueled the American dream – that most of us can achieve comfortable and prosperous lives if we make a steady climb up the ladder, without necessarily having to reach the top. By setting our sights on the top rung, we can't see that the middle rung is being taken away from us, and the middle class is losing its footing.

Most important, we continue to believe that our political process, so much of which revolves around prolonged seasons of campaign rhetoric leading up to the ritual of voting on Election Day, is really about change. We continue to believe that the process will bring about the kind of change we want, the kind of change we need, the kind of change that will benefit most of the people.

There are precedents in American history that allow us to believe this. We saw real change in 1932, when

Franklin Delano Roosevelt defeated Herbert Hoover. The financial markets had crashed, and during the Great Depression great masses of people were unemployed. The new FDR government regulated the markets and created jobs and social-welfare nets.

These measures began the process of recovery, but the massive federal deficit spending during World War II – $53 billion in 1943 – was the primary factor in turning the Depression-era economy around.[3] After the war Harry Truman expanded the GI Bill, which has enabled countless numbers of Americans to achieve higher education, Americans who otherwise wouldn't have had that chance.

We saw real change again during the Kennedy-Johnson years, when the government took an active role in fighting poverty and promoting civil rights. Once again, by virtue of real political change, more of us gained opportunities that put the American dream within our reach.

We have seen in our history that the political process can take the country in a direction that changes things for the better for many people. But today we have reached a point where the political process changes the parties in power but does not deliver the kind of change that will allow most of us to achieve, or hold on to, the American dream.

In my 42 years of public service as a legislator, judge and regulator, I have come to understand some of the key reasons this has happened. It has happened because we no longer have the direct connection to our politics that we once had, due primarily to the degree that moneyed interests have come between the people and their representatives in government.

It has happened because those who represent us in government increasingly take the easy way out, and in most cases this means that political expediency trumps good public policy.

And it has happened because we the people have lost the ability to listen to one another inside and outside the halls of power. In our own Babelian way, we have imposed a listening deficit on our political culture that poses as much risk to us as do the budgetary deficits that plague all levels of government.

For all of these reasons, real change – as opposed to the appearance of change – has become a commodity that is much, much harder to achieve through our political process. Real change is no longer the natural outcome of new candidates stepping up to the plate, winning the confidence of voters, assuming office and renewing the direction that our country takes. In short, achieving real change is no longer a simple matter of throwing the bums out every few years.

By convincing ourselves that it's change enough until the next election, that putting in a new cast of characters every two or four years is sufficient to get the job done, we have put ourselves and our American dream at great risk. If there is a lesson to be learned from the elections of 2008 and 2010, it is not that the people have spoken and that change is on the way.

Rather, the lesson – which we are not hearing about on the 24/7 networks – is that we cannot afford to keep kidding ourselves and indulging in Babel-speak. We have to cut through the babble of slogans including "get the government off our backs" and "change we can believe in" and get to the bottom line. We have to ask ourselves: Why are we risking our American dream?

Regaining the social cohesion that we need in order to have a national conversation won't be easy. American society has changed greatly since the term "American dream" came into vogue, and we can't turn the clock back. Communications technology and the structure of the economy are completely different today than they were back then.

When I was a kid in Lawndale there were no computers or jet airplanes. Because we didn't have the distraction of television or the comfort of air conditioning, we spent more time outdoors than kids do today.

On hot summer nights we would go to Douglas Park to catch the breeze, or we stood on the corner with friends and talked. When we walked down Independence Boulevard we saw people sitting on their stoops. People knew one another, and they talked to one another.

People were motivated to take care of one another. Kids knew better than to step out of line, because respect was important. You respected your parents, you respected your teachers. I didn't dare come home and tell my parents that I had a disagreement with Madame Wahl, my Spanish teacher at Marshall High School. If I had, Karl and Dora would have said: "So what did you do wrong?"

When I rode the streetcar down Roosevelt Road, I knew I had to give up my seat if an elderly person was standing. That was built into us; you had to have respect for your fellow human being. We knew that doing the right thing was its own reward.

Parents always knew that their kids were being watched by the mothers in the neighborhood. If I was out with my friends Milton and Louie and something happened to one of us, it was a good bet that one of our mothers would take charge right away. For the same reason, we watched how we behaved, because there was always someone in the neighborhood looking after us. The neighborhood was like a big family.

When you went to the Karl Jaffe Tailor Shop, it wasn't only a business visit. It was a social visit. You walked into my father's shop and you'd run into a priest from St. Finbarr's. Officer Hoff, the cop who patrolled our neighborhood and lived there too, might be engaged in conversation with Morris the butcher, an Orthodox Jew who was not only a purveyor of fine kosher meats but also the cantor at his synagogue. They would all come by the tailor shop even when they didn't need their trousers pressed or let out, because every place of business on Pulaski Road was a meeting place.

Next door to my father's shop was Abie's Barber Shop. It had two red leather chairs, but Abie always seated his customers in the one closest to the front door. When I would go in for a haircut, I never had an appointment; no one did. You came in and you waited.

As a kid I would sit in the barber chair and Abie would say to me: "Write a letter for me." He would dictate a missive to his relatives in Europe, and I would sit and write as he cut my hair. I never did ask Abie whether he knew how to write.

In the back of Abie's shop was a room where insurance salesmen hung out. They went to Abie's to sit and talk, and everyone knew that they would play cards in the back room. Abie didn't care, because no one else was using the back room anyway.

One day a police officer came in and said to Abie: "I'm going to arrest you because you're running a gambling parlor." And Abie said: "What kind of gambling parlor are you talking about?"

Cop: "There are guys playing cards in the back room."

Abie: "Well, of course. They always do that."

Cop: "How much money do you make off them?"

Abie: "That's silly, they always play cards. I don't make a penny."

Cop: "If you don't tell me, I'm going to arrest you."

And Abie said: "Call your captain, because he comes in here and plays cards with the insurance guys too."

And then the police officer said: "Really?" And he slunk off.

There was always a discussion going on. Every possible philosophy got an airing in the tailor shop, the barber shop, the butcher shop. Everyone was talking, from the hard-line capitalist who never had a penny in his pocket to the self-styled socialist who would tell you that come the revolution, we were all going to eat strawberries.

In effect, a national conversation was happening. People didn't sit transfixed playing with gadgets; we didn't have them. A daily exercise was taking place, and from it emerged ... life. You could hear the ideas bubbling to the surface.

We didn't interact differently with one another only on the street. We also had a different relationship with those whom we elected to represent us. Although politics has always had its intrigues and shady characters, back then, for the most part, it was considered a noble profession.

A person doing good public service was thought of highly. In those days politics had a certain morality all its own. A politician's private life was private, and what mattered was whether he carrying out his duty and how well was he performing his job.

Today every conceivable detail of a politician's life is taken into account. This has a terrible consequence: Many good people are discouraged from going into politics because to run for office means that you have to be on public exhibit 24 hours a day, and everyone has the right to know every detail about your life.

If a politician is corrupt or engages in other behavior that has a negative impact on his conduct in office, that's one thing. But what's it anyone's business when political figures have personal financial problems or when their kids get into trouble, unless these factors hinder officeholders from doing what they were elected to do?

I can't remember my parents ever talking about a politician's private life. Back in the day, if someone had told my father that FDR was having an extramarital affair, Karl Jaffe would have said: "What's it your business? He's the president – let him do his job."

When I was growing up in Lawndale we had a direct line to our elected representatives. Sy Siegel was the precinct captain, and he was a kind of ombudsman for the community. From time to time the doorbell would ring, and Sy would be there.

Sy's job was to get out the vote in the precinct. He would come around to talk to the people, but he would do it all year round, not just at election time. Part politico and part social worker, he would find out what people needed. Was there a pothole in the street, a crack in the sidewalk? Did someone need another garbage can? Was someone sick?

If you had a problem that was beyond Sy's ability to solve, such as a water bill that was too high, he would make an appointment for you or take you down to see the alderman or ward committeeman, who would then contact the water company to check the meter and see what could be done. If there was a mistake, they would work on straightening it out. The whole idea was to serve the people.

When a holiday came and someone didn't have the resources to celebrate in a proper fashion, Sy would bring over a turkey or a chicken to make sure that no one would go hungry. The bottom line was to get your vote. But the politicians were there to serve you and to make sure that the government served you.

The American dream emerged amid this social cohesion. The American dream used to be that you could get an education, you could get a job and buy a house, you could take care of your family. You could go on vacation and live a life of relative prosperity. People had faith in the idea that if you worked hard and did your job and were sincere, then you would have a good chance of accomplishing what you wanted to accomplish.

Today that has gone out the window for many people who don't have jobs and are losing their houses. Higher education is getting tougher and tougher to afford. In the American dream, you could have a pension if you worked hard and put some money away. Today pensions of all kinds are dwindling and disappearing.

The American dream took place in a friendlier world, a place where relationships were built on trust. If you wanted a mortgage or other type of loan, you would talk to a banker. She would advise you and try to help you as best she could, and sometimes she would take a chance on you.

Today your credit rating is determined by a computer programmed with formulas devised by people whom you don't know and can't see. You go into a bank, and there's a lot of empty space because so many employees have been replaced by ATMs and online banking. In the old days, the bank officers were there. Today they are corporate executives who are someplace far away.

In America today the human being has been beaten down more than a little bit. Our humanity has been diminished. We are no longer simply struggling to get the better things in life. Many of us are struggling to keep our heads above water.

In June 2011 the U.S. Department of Labor released data showing that over the last decade, the share of national income taken home by American workers has hit a record low. The slide started with the short recession that followed Sept. 11, 2001, and it continued even as the economy picked up again, worsening when the Great Recession hit. In the weak recovery since then, workers' share of income has continued to drop.[4]

Analysts have attributed the trend to factors including the decline in the bargaining power of labor and the rise in competition from foreign workers. While American companies enjoyed record profits in 2010-2011, unemployment remained high and wages barely rose.[5] All the while, there hasn't been much talk coming out of the White House or Congress about this growing inequality.

So whose American dream is it? Does the American dream of the 21st century belong only to those who become super-rich beyond imagination? Or does it belong to all Americans, who should have an equal chance at reasonable levels of prosperity? Does the American dream belong only to the privileged few at the top, while the rest of us become bamboozled cheerleaders on the sidelines and many are being pushed to the margins?

If ever there was a time of trickle-down wealth, it is no more. The poor are getting poorer faster than ever before, the super-rich are becoming super-richer, and there are fewer people in the middle. The small business owner is in danger of becoming extinct. Today the tone and tenor of our economy is determined by big corporations that slice jobs relentlessly and reward their top executives with extraordinary levels of compensation.

This state of affairs has sapped our collective energy. Not too long ago Americans were known the world over for our can-do attitude, but that confidence has been eroded. The forces against us are so strong that many of us have become resigned to just riding the tide. But this isn't the time to ride the tide; it's the time to fight it.

The happy warrior optimism that I have had for most of my life is diminished but not dead. It will be revitalized when I see America become America again. It will be revitalized when the people remember that the government belongs to them and they take the steps to get it back.

My father's sense of the American dream led him to believe that each succeeding generation would build a higher floor of the house. Today Karl would say that we are stuck between floors and that we need to jolt ourselves into getting on with construction. We need to generate our own power so we can continue to build the house of our dreams, the house in which succeeding generations will have things at least as good as we do if not better.

Only two generations ago, Americans created a society that was the first of its kind. Most of the people were on their way to having a lifestyle that was not only more affluent but much happier than those enjoyed by people in many other countries around the world. And the world admired us, not only for our standard of living but also for the iterations of the American dream that we created – those magical Hollywood musicals and our walk on the moon, to name but two.

Today the American dream is about not giving up on being the best that we can be. We need to think about how we used to be and what we've done, not for the sake of nostalgia but to guide our way forward.

Forward thinking is especially important for young Americans, because they will lose the most if the American dream disappears. If this sense of vision is left to baby boomers and seniors, they may very well be the last generations to have built and hung on to the higher floors of the house.

The bumper stickers might say: Fight for change. Get your hands dirty. Wishing won't make it so. Hopeless = Powerless. But we have to go way beyond slogans and sound bites.

We have to ask: What are we gaining by letting the American dream slip away? Are we ready to become the people who preside over the end of the American dream as once we knew it?

Like any time travelers, Karl and Dora would be quite perplexed if they were to be transported to another era, namely the America of today. But they would make no bones about what they would see. What would surprise them most is not the evidence of material progress that American society has made. Rather, they would be taken aback by how our social cohesion has come unglued and how passively most of us are reacting to the predicament we now face.

They would notice immediately that most hair salons of today are no longer places to relax and have a conversation. At the gas station, they would observe not only that gas costs a small fortune but also that nobody pumps it for you anymore.

At the grocery store, they would see the self-pay stations that have idled many of the cash-register lanes where people actually bag your groceries. They would notice right away that in the self-pay line you give a computer your money and bag the items yourself. Again, there's no one to talk to.

Some might argue that given the choice, people will opt for lower prices over personal service. But some choices we make; others we don't. The lack of service and human contact are more often than not chosen for us.

My father would shake his head and say "America *goniff*," a Yiddish expression he used in the old days when someone wasn't acting appropriately, when someone was cutting corners, when someone was employing sneaky tactics to get money out of you – the way things didn't used to happen in the old country. Today his "America *goniff*" would translate roughly to: "We just want your money. As far as being concerned about you, forget about it."

Dora used to go to the movies to see Jeanette MacDonald and Nelson Eddy in a beautiful love story. She would read Yiddish romance novels. But she knew what was entertainment and what was politics.

Today she would watch the soap operas constructed around the private lives of politicians and she would ask: "Why are you looking for entertainment in the place where you should be looking for answers to your problems?"

Karl never owned a car. When we would ride the streetcar, he would look out the window and say: "Look at all those cars. You would think they cost a nickel apiece." He was a tailor who made cuffs for a quarter, and he had a sense of wonder at how prosperous people could become.

Today he would see even more cars on the street, but he would be more interested in all the empty storefronts and the "bank owned" signs in front of so many houses. He would ask: "What's going on? What happened? You were supposed to make things better!"

He would be amazed by the sense of quiet resignation that so many Americans have about the precarious downturn the economy has taken. He would be puzzled by what led to the crash of '08. "Hey, wait a minute," he would say, "didn't Roosevelt straighten this thing out a long time ago when he curbed the power of the banks? But today they have become the big shots of the economy.

"Where is the small-business owner," Karl would ask, "the guy who builds up a business so his family can be comfortable? Why are so many of those smaller stores closed? And why do you need all of these big stores, when there's no one in them to wait on you?

"We went through the Depression and fought two world wars to make America better and safer," Karl Jaffe the straight talker would say. "I came to America in order to build a life for myself and my family. Here I attained what I could not attain in the place I was born. But here you are today, with everything turned on its head."

And then he would come in for the kill.

"Have you gone *meshuga*?" he would ask, using the Yiddish word for crazy.

"Is this the way things are going to be, or is this *mishegas*" – this craziness –"only temporary?"

In Greece, protestors came out by the thousands in May 2010 to decry their country's economic crisis. In France the following October, when the government proposed raising the retirement age from 60 to 62, citizens took to the streets to protest.

In Arab countries throughout North Africa and the Middle East, throngs led by young people have taken to the streets from Tunis to Cairo to Sana'a to Damascus since December 2010 to demand an end to the autocracy and corruption of decades-old regimes.

The economic and political contexts that spurred these protests are different from the context that imperils our American dream. But the ethos of these international protests is important all the same: In these countries people have been moved to take action when they believed their vital interests were threatened by the powers that be.

In America some people have decided that the time has come for taking our grievances to the streets. The Wisconsin labor protests that began in February 2011 were the first indication of this shift; the Occupy Wall Street movement that burst on the scene the following September is undeniable proof that something new has started to happen.

Have we reached the tipping point? Is this what is compelling thousands of Americans, like citizens in Athens and Paris and Cairo, to stage ongoing demonstrations across the country and to put our leaders on notice?

Americans are confronted with critical issues in our everyday lives but until recently haven't begun to react to them collectively. Take the price of gasoline. In the summer of 2010, the price of regular gas in the Chicago metropolitan area averaged around $3 gallon. By early summer 2011, the price had skyrocketed to between $4.25 and $4.50 a gallon – an increase approaching 50 percent within a year's time during a still-weak national economy. While gas prices in the Chicago area are among the highest in the country, proportional spikes occurred from coast to coast. What happened?

We are told that global demand is increasing steadily, constantly driving prices up. But did the demand for gas by people in emerging-market economies such as China,

India and Brazil increase proportionally by 50 percent over the course of that same year?

Then we were told that the unrest of the Arab spring sparked fears of shortages. But the only major oil-producing Arab country to experience significant and prolonged unrest has been Libya, which supplies only about 2 percent of global oil demand and a minuscule one-half of 1 percent of daily U.S. oil imports.[6]

What happened, as we were compelled to shell out more for gas and for all goods transported by gas-burning vehicles, had less to do with what was happening in Beijing and Mumbai and Tripoli than it did with what was transpiring on Wall Street, in lower Manhattan, New York City.

There, speculators have been driving up oil prices by betting on them in unregulated oil-futures markets[7] and lining their pockets while the rest of us have had to empty ours out faster at the pump and the grocery store.

The hum of big bucks being made has also reverberated in the boardrooms of oil companies, which chalked up record profits in 2010 and 2011. While many sectors of our recession-battered economy continued to lag and gas prices averaged $4 a gallon at the beginning of 2011, first-quarter earnings for ExxonMobil, BP, Shell, Chevron and ConocoPhillips were $34 billion, up 42 percent from 2010.

According to *The Huffington Post*, "That's about $110 for every man, woman and child in the United States – in just three months. Exxon alone cleared a cool $10.7 billion profit from January through March [2011], up 69 percent from 2010. That's $82,175 a minute."[8]

Meanwhile, the price of gas within any metropolitan region of the United States is basically the same, no matter what oil company is selling it. Where is the competition? Where are the antitrust laws regulating oil-company profits?

Did the government investigate whether there was price rigging? Has anyone in the White House or Congress proposed that the price of gasoline should be regulated during the present period of economic crisis, as the federal government did at various times in decades past by imposing production and price controls on the U.S. petroleum industry?[9]

I drive down the main streets and see vacant storefront after vacant storefront. I don't hear the American people talking about that. But I do hear the 24/7 newspeople talking about the supposed economic recovery and how low interest rates are. But the question is: low for whom?

Interest is low for the big banks, which borrow money from the Federal Reserve for less than 1 percent. But the banks don't pass that rate on to consumers. The banks issue credit cards with interest rates that are in the double digits and go as high as 29 percent.

The highest interest rates are charged to the people who can least afford to pay them. Large corporations get low interest rates, but a working poor person who is barely able to pay her monthly bills may have to pay 29 percent interest. Where's the outcry about that? Where's the justice in that?

Meanwhile, the recession has been said to be technically over, but the banks are still very slow to approve mortgages, and people are still losing their houses. If you do have a mortgage and are one day late on your payment – or on your credit-card payment – the banks sock you with fees and penalties.

If you call the credit-card company, first you'll talk to a computer. Then the first live person you will speak to, the person who is representing an American bank, is likely to answer your call from somewhere in Asia. If you have a complaint about your account, you are routed to the lowest person in the chain of command, and that person tells you that nothing can be done.

If you persist you are transferred to another person who will tell you the same thing. After a while many Americans give up on calling, because there's no one who will serve you. Banking is supposed to be a service industry, but whom do the banks really serve?

Once upon a time, there was a department store called Marshall Field's, which was founded in Chicago. It was famous for its array of beautiful goods, but it was equally well-known for the way it did business. The company's hallmark mottos were: "Give the lady what she wants" and "The customer is always right." When customers had complaints, they got service. And most of the time that service was in the customers' favor.

Not many companies still do businesses that way today. When you go into a department store or a grocery store or a pharmacy, you often have a tough time finding a cashier station that is open or a clerk to help you find an item on the sales floor.

The arrogance of capital, which plagues the American consumer in myriad ways, has been enabled from the top down. The original intent of corporations was for people to be able to invest in businesses without taking a high degree of individual risk. In recent years Congress and the Supreme Court have deemed that corporations are just like people. But this, in effect, has come to mean that corporations now have more rights than people do.

There was a time when people could deduct the interest they paid on credit-card balances from their income taxes. Thanks to Congress, people can't do that anymore, but corporations can deduct interest payments as a cost of doing business.

There was a time when only people had freedom of speech. Now the Supreme Court has taken limits off corporate campaign financing on the theory that such donations are a form of free speech.

When individuals go through bankruptcy, they have to undergo a thorough examination to see if they qualify, and being in bankruptcy leaves a mark on a person's credit rating for years. Corporations, on the other hand, can declare bankruptcy relatively easily in order to write off onerous debt or to restructure – and then continue doing business with little or no stigma. Corporations undergo bankruptcy as if it were financial plastic surgery; for mere people, on the other hand, it's more like a traumatic, lifesaving operation.

One way or another, most Americans are increasingly exposed to having the deck stacked against us in these various ways. The government is compliant, the corporate-owned mainstream media are silent and there seems to be no public outrage. This ultimately wears away the social cohesion that is needed to effect change.

By the time Americans walk away from the gas pump and hang up the phone with the credit-card company and finish standing in line at the store, we are exhausted and overcome with frustration.

What are we supposed to do amid this frustration, this exhaustion, this sense that the problems are too overwhelming and there's nothing that can be done? How can we change things to start reversing our national course so we can hang on to the American dream?

Perhaps we should take a cue from the growing number of Americans who have started to stand up collectively like people in France, like people in Greece, like people in so many Arab countries who have made revolutions and are demanding change.

Street protests are an important first step, but they are only a first step. We know what ails us. Now we need a plan of action. Having lived my own American dream, which has included four decades in public service, I believe the plan of action should go something like this:

First, in order to hold on to the American dream, we have some major reclamation work to do. This work starts in our hearts and minds. We must visualize not only what is necessary but also what is possible.

A crucial element of this visualization is reclaiming our sense of destiny. We have to believe that we control our own destiny and that we're not helpless. Today there's a widespread feeling out there of "What am I going to do? There's nothing I can do." But we're not helpless, because according to the Constitution of the United States, power lies in the hands of the people. We are the government.

Then we have to reclaim our government. We have to re-energize ourselves to participate in political life actively, from the local level on up, and to work within the system to make it better. If the political parties aren't giving us what we want, then we have to find a different breed of candidates and think seriously about expanding our two-party system.

After that we have to be ready to reclaim our economy. We need to understand that we have to take back the Treasury Department, which for some time has been run by people who are or have been intimately associated with the banks and investment houses. We can't have the friends of the people who are being regulated doing the regulating. It's that simple. It's worse than the inmates running the asylum.

We must also be ready to demand that our lawmakers enforce the antitrust laws that are on the books. We cannot allow corporations to get so big that the government deems they are too big to fail. And we have to put a much higher price on white-collar financial crimes. America has the biggest prison population in the world, but we have yet to bring to trial, much less to prison, the people who hijacked the American economy in recent years.

The last item on the reclamation agenda is to recapture our sense of the future. We cannot continue to be mesmerized by quick, short-term fixes. For example, there's a trend in this country to privatize things that government used to do.

In 2005 the city of Chicago privatized the Chicago Skyway, the 7.8-mile toll road that links Chicago to Indiana, in order to get a cash infusion of $1.8 billion. This was the first privatization of an existing toll road anywhere in the United States. Chicago gave a private Spanish-Australian consortium a 99-year lease not only to operate and maintain the Skyway but also to pocket its toll and concession revenues.[10]

However, if an international joint venture can run the road for its own profit, why can't the local government do it to profit the people? That $1.8 billion was a good chunk of money, and it solved some immediate revenue problems. But when the chunk is gone – and it won't last 99 years – the private company will still be making a profit for decades to come, and the city will look for other quick fixes.

After visualization, political mobilization comes next in the plan of action. We need to start by getting beyond the rhetoric of "throw the bums out" and avoiding the pitfalls of replacing those bums with new bums who are equally bad if not worse. We have to jump-start our political system, which has become stagnant and unresponsive.

We have to look closely at whom the existing parties are running for office. When faced with candidates who are indebted to the same powers that have brought this country to the brink of disaster, we have to say "No more!" and find a different breed of challengers.

We can't do that by sitting at home in front of the computer or TV. We have to hit the streets and organize, go door to door and be prepared for a fight. Those who know how to organize – including unions that represent teachers and public employees – are being discredited by forces that don't have the public interest at heart.

In this day and age we have more channels for venting than ever before, whether we're following the pundits on myriad websites and cable networks or doing the venting ourselves by blogging and texting and tweeting. But venting doesn't change the system.

If you and your candidate get a group of people together to picket JPMorgan Chase, on the other hand, then you force the media to shine a spotlight on your message. The media care about getting an audience. So we have to be adventurous and play the system. Political theater can put a principled message across.

This is no game, though; it couldn't be more serious. We seem to have forgotten the simplest concept: Our representatives are supposed to represent us. But to a worrisome degree, they're not doing that anymore;

they're representing those who fill their campaign coffers. That doesn't promote democracy; it promotes oligarchy. And in recent years we have begun to pay the painful price that the oligarchs exact. We have got to act in order to change things.

We should not stop at reinvigorating the existing political parties, however. We need an inclusive ingathering where the left and the right and the center are talking to one another.

This could be achieved by a movement to create a bona fide Independent Party of the center. At present there are only two independent members of Congress, Senators Joe Lieberman and Bernie Sanders. But there is nothing holy about having only two parties, especially when they are not delivering what we need. Many democracies in advanced capitalist countries support not just two political parties but three or more.

A full-fledged Independent Party would allow its members to vote their principles according to the merits of the issues. An Independent Party could serve as a bridge of pragmatism between the right and the left. An Independent Party would also put the Democrats and Republicans on notice that they have to work together for the public good to stay relevant, and that gridlock is not an option when there's a mediating force and an alternative political address in the center.

In the national conversation we must have, we need to ask ourselves what we really want, and we have to examine our priorities and our methods very closely. On the right, this process has been led by the Tea Party.

It has succeeded in organizing conservatives across the country, in groups big and small. The Tea Party brought people out to the streets and discussed their ideas – often in loud, angry voices – and then took action. In 2010 it successfully ran candidates and started to change the American political landscape. The Tea Party has shaken up the system by getting people together, pushing ideas and objecting to the status quo.

Before I go any further, I must qualify my view of the Tea Party: I do not agree with many of the positions it espouses. The major difference between the Tea Party and me is that in some areas of public policy, I favor more government, not less.

But before we can agree on the substance, we have to address the method. The Tea Party gets it; the Tea Party gets the method. Tea Partiers know how to mobilize people and rally them for change. Tea Partiers understand that they have to organize, they understand that they have to make noise, they understand that they have to fight.

So far, though, most of what the Tea Party has generated is a show of anger.

That's only a starting point. The Tea Party is still summoning slogans instead of addressing the core of the issues. It has installed a new cast of characters in Congress but has yet to lay the groundwork for solving problems. It has stirred things up on the surface, but the depths remain murky. The moneyed interests are still hijacking the process of government by and for the people.

The Tea Party has to come up with solutions. It can't be satisfied merely with electing candidates who can't or won't change the status quo in a way that benefits the many instead of the few. The Tea Party will have to deal with the issues in depth, but it has succeeded in jump-starting the mechanisms of engagement.

The left has begun to respond. The Occupy Wall Street movement has gained considerable momentum with its street protests across the country, and it has articulated a slate of issues. Then there's the Coffee Party,[11] a caffeine-inspired answer to the Tea Party from the left. Fueled by civic engagement of re-energized Americans, all of these groups across the political spectrum have to start talking to one another in order to find a modus vivendi that will move our society forward.

The truth of the matter is that while the right and the left are far apart on the substance of the big issues, their ultimate goals are basically the same. Both want a government that is responsive and accountable to the people, a government that is by and for the people. We have lost that and we need to reclaim it – from the left, from the right and from the center.

The last step in the plan of action is implementation. We have to work for concrete policy changes that are based on the idea that our government needs to get back to the business of serving the people.

The most crucial form of government intervention that we need is a comprehensive re-regulation of the financial system. The Dodd-Frank financial reform act of 2010 marked the beginning of the process, but this reform does not go far enough. Congress must reinstate the strict and unambiguous separation of commercial and investment banking provided by the Glass-Steagall Act of 1933.

We need the government to get *on* – not off – the backs of the big banks, investment houses and insurance companies to make sure they play fair and are not able to put the financial futures of average Americans at risk the way they did leading up to the crash of 2008.

The next step is to reprioritize the distribution of our national resources, in particular military spending. I will say it plainly: We cannot put our national security at risk. But we have to undertake an honest re-evaluation about what's needed to protect the United States.

Moreover, we can't wage war and pretend it isn't war. The conditions laid down in the Constitution for sending our troops to fight overseas cannot be circumvented. When the president intends to commit American men, women and materiel to engage in battle, he has to ask Congress to declare war.

Until the recent economic meltdown, it has been an axiom that the one area of the federal budget that could never be cut was military spending. However, the Great Recession has apparently forced our leaders to begin to take a hard look at reality – prompting them to cut a modest $78 billion in projected military spending through 2016. This is the first retraction in U.S. military spending since the beginning of the Cold War immediately after World War II.[12]

We have to come up with a formula that strikes a better balance between projecting our military power and effecting prudent policies to defend our country and to maintain constructive relationships with the rest of the world. Then we have to be prepared to make further cuts in our military budget accordingly.

The savings from those cuts should immediately be channeled to social spending on health care and education. They should also be reallocated in part to research and development and worker retraining that create living-wage jobs in fields such as information technology, biotechnology and energy technology – jobs that do not leave our shores.

Job creation is key to growing our economy, and growth is the only way to keep the government adequately funded without resorting to massive tax hikes and slashing social and entitlement programs.

Just as deregulation of the American financial industry has imperiled the American dream, so has the evaporation of domestic manufacturing in the United States. From the mid-19th to the mid-20th century, the industrialization of America, along with the creation of the federal interstate highway system and the resulting suburban sprawl, contributed greatly to the expansion of the American dream.

Yet with every American factory shuttered over the last 30 years, and with every manufacturing and (in more recent years) service job that has migrated overseas, the American dream continues to contract.

There are various schools of thought about how and to what extent American manufacturing can be revived. Economic globalization is inevitable and inexorable, as evidenced by the expansion and privatization of the Chinese economy and other emerging market economies over the last three decades.

Free from government regulation, American corporations have been active partners in this global phenomenon. They have seized the opportunity to maximize profits by slashing domestic manufacturing. They have capitalized on rock-bottom labor costs of offshore production and high sales volumes generated by cheaper goods manufactured overseas.

While on the surface these bargains may seem like a win-win scenario for American business and consumers alike, there is a considerable economic cost to the current imbalance between offshore production and domestic manufacturing. Maximizing profits by producing and selling goods at the lowest possible cost is proving to be not only narrow-minded but also short-sighted.

Simply put, there's a viable economic basis for doing business another way. The cumulative costs of massive American job loss brought on by the shift away from domestic manufacturing over the last three decades have never been clearer than they are today.

Outsourcing and downsizing dry up not only employment but also consumer spending and associated revenues in the form of sales and income taxes. The revenue crisis, in turn, affects us all in the form of reduced government services and even fewer available jobs. American jobs, even at higher labor costs, generate revenue that supports the entire economy.

It's a virtual certainty that many would greet the idea of government-mandated domestic-manufacturing goals for American businesses with alarmed cries of "Socialism!" But in reality it would be in our own national security and economic interests to find ways to incentivize domestic manufacture of a percentage of everything that we consume.

Goals could be set for domestic production of each category of consumer goods, with tax breaks for manufacturing in America a percentage of all goods sold in America.

For example, such legislation could require a certain percentage of all clothing that Walmart and other giant retailers sell to be produced in the United States. These retailers and the manufacturers that supply them would then have the option of meeting the target and qualifying for a tax break or paying a relatively higher tax rate on profits from sales of imported goods.

In other words, the government would offer an incentive for doing business a certain way, and it would be up to businesses to choose.

After getting the financial industry under control and shifting resources from military spending to social spending and job creation (including revising the tax codes to incentivize domestic manufacturing), we need to come up with a national plan and individual state plans to reverse our disastrous course of deficit spending and borrowing.

We have to find a way to live within our means and to stop mortgaging the future of our country. We must have policies we can pay for as we go. But this cannot be done on the backs of working people by using union-busting tactics.

We also have to jump on the third rail of taxes. We must restructure our tax system to be more equitable; to eliminate loopholes that bolster the corporate bottom line while depriving the federal and state governments of much-needed revenue; to strike a better balance between how individuals are taxed and how corporations are taxed.

We must also put a permanent end to tax cuts that greatly favor those individuals in the top few percentiles. We cannot wait for prosperity to trickle down. We all need a shot at prosperity from the bottom up.

And in the mix, we need to accept the plain reality that after taking these steps, there just might be some things left on our national wish list for which we will have to agree to pay higher taxes.

Finally, we must find solutions to campaign-finance reform. Because such reform is likely to be obstructed in the near term by the Supreme Court in the wake of its landmark *Citizens United* decision of 2010, the approach should be twofold. First, we need mandatory public funding of federal campaigns so that candidates will limit their spending in return for government funding, thereby greatly reducing the amount of money they need to raise from private donors.

Second, along lines that the Occupy movement has proposed, we need to push for a constitutional amendment that will take virtual citizenship and free-speech rights away from corporations, effectively reversing *Citizens United*.

So this is the plan of action: visualize, mobilize, implement. We can no longer afford just to sit back, point our fingers at others and say: "Those guys are liberals, conservatives, capitalists, socialists ... and they're bad." We are still stoking our arguments with terms that came into vogue in the 19th century. We need to throw out those outdated "isms" and focus on the thing that we all have in common.

And that thing is the American dream.

We can't solve the equation without doing the math. We can't lose the 20 pounds without going on the diet. We can't fix our problems without having the national conversation, without having the tea and coffee parties and without bringing them together to get America back on track.

In the wake of the Tucson shootings in January 2011, which struck down Congresswoman Gabrielle Giffords and killed six other Americans, President Obama consoled the nation. He spoke of the national conversation that had already started about civility in public discourse.

Obama counseled that "only a more civil and honest public discourse can help us face up to our challenges as a nation." He admonished that "we can question each other's ideas without questioning each other's love of country, and that our task, working together, is to constantly widen the circle of our concern so that we bequeath the American dream to future generations."[13]

However, we can little afford to heed such notions only in times of tragedy, reverting to our usual ways once the headlines change and our attention is diverted elsewhere.

Back in 1976, in his film masterpiece *Network*, Paddy Chayefsky implored Americans to get up, open their windows, stick out their heads and yell: "I'm as mad as hell, and I'm not going to take this anymore!"

Today we have mastered the art of shouting out the window, but we have not figured out what to do next. What we need to do next is to stop shouting and have a national conversation that brings people together across the gamut of political viewpoints.

We need to get the right and the left and the center back into the public square. To do this we should mine the capabilities of the virtual world, but at the same time we must appreciate its limits. This will be one among many challenges for young Americans, who are masters of virtual-world technology.

We can and should use social networking constructively as a tool to galvanize public discourse. But social networking should not become a substitute for the discourse itself.

We can use Twitter and Facebook to mobilize, but at some point we also have to be ready to idle our computers, put down our cellphones and get out there in the square and talk to one another face to face. We need to start talking in our neighborhoods, in supermarkets, in high school and college auditoriums, in city council chambers – wherever we gather.

The starting point of the conversation will be that the system isn't working, and that if we let the system fail for too long, then we will have to say goodbye, American dream.

That realization will energize us, and then real change can start to happen. But that change has to happen in the three-dimensional world.

If you have a serious illness, you can find lots of helpful background information about your medical condition on the Internet. But to get the treatment and the cure that you need, you have to meet the physician face to face.

And then you may have to show up at the hospital. You may have to lie down on the operating table and let the doctor put her hands deep into your guts so she can cure what ails you.

The American dream is worth fighting for.

It is worth fighting for because we still have human values. We still want to live a life that's free, a life in which we are free to think and say whatever we want to say. A life in which we can make a living and provide for our families no matter what type of families they may be. We want to make sure that when we're older, we will be taken care of, that we will have the health care we're going to need.

Regardless of how technology advances, popular culture evolves and styles change, some things are timeless. The American dream isn't a fad whose time has come and gone. It is a promise of a way of life that transcends fashion. The dream does not become dated, like music and clothing styles, or outdated, like electronic gadgetry. This is because the basic things that we need to live stable, prosperous lives really don't change.

The American dream is worth fighting for because it's a human dream. It's not computer generated. It's a dream for human advancement and human thought and human comfort and human security.

The American dream isn't a TV show that if it gets canceled, something else will replace it next season. The American dream is a basis for human fulfillment, a promise of a way forward.

The American dream is something many Americans will miss, because it's something many of us already have. Once it's gone, we're not going to be able to live the life to which we've become accustomed.

Already opportunities to advance within American society are dwindling. The rich have become richer, the middle class is struggling to stay in the middle and the poor are in worse shape. The American dream is worth fighting for because it represents the life we already have come to expect.

Young Americans have the most to lose if the American dream evaporates, but they also have the greatest and most inspiring challenge ahead of them to save it.

What made the men and women of the "greatest generation" of the 20th century great was that they suffered the trials of the Great Depression and then during WWII, on foreign soil and in the war effort at home, fought to preserve our freedom in the face of threats that emanated from outside our borders.

The test of greatness for the young men and women who have come of age during the Great Recession of the early 21st century will be to demand – and then to implement – the changes it will take to save the American dream from threats that have originated from within our borders.

If you're a young American today, it's important to know that the American dream is not pie in the sky or some abstract concept from the past that is no longer relevant. The American dream is not the stuff of nostalgia. It is the stuff of necessity if we want to preserve what we have.

If you know someone who came to the United States from another country and has become an American citizen, then you have witnessed the American dream.

If you know someone who has gotten unemployment compensation after being was laid off from work, or someone who is the first in his or her family to earn a college degree, then you have observed evidence of the American dream.

If you know someone who can't afford health insurance but who has received medical treatment through Medicare or Medicaid, then you have seen the American dream at work.

On the other hand, if you know that increasing numbers of people in your community are now going to food pantries and soup kitchens, then you have seen signs of the American dream unraveling.

If you have seen somebody who has had her house foreclosed, then you know that the American dream can disappear.

If you have seen the value of your family's retirement funds dwindle in recent years to proportions that no longer reflect the years of hard work that it took to build those savings, then you understand how deregulated financial markets have endangered and will continue to endanger the American dream.

Recently I ate lunch at a coffee shop where my server, who does not earn a high salary, looked rather pale and sick. I asked her what was the matter, and she told me that she had a stomach ailment and had been in pain most of the night before.

When she went to the local emergency room, she told the clerk that she has no health insurance; he asked her how she was going to pay for treatment. This woman, who works double shifts in a restaurant to support her children, couldn't get the care she needed. She left the hospital with nothing but a prescription for medication that cost $200, which she couldn't afford.

This is what happens when the American dream fails.

Even though we are hearing more and more of such stories, I remain hopeful. I find hope in the fact that the government of our country still belongs to us. It belongs to the people. When I need to remind myself of that, I go to the source. I take out my pocket guide to the U.S. Constitution, and I read the preamble, which states:

We the People of the United States, in Order to form a more perfect Union, establish Justice, insure domestic Tranquility, provide for the common defence, promote the general Welfare, and secure the Blessings of Liberty to ourselves and our Posterity, do ordain and establish this Constitution for the United States of America.

The preamble talks only about the people. It does not talk about banks, investment houses or insurance companies. The Constitution was written by and for real people. It was written for you and me, for the citizens of this country. It is more than just theory, even if the practice has become somewhat distorted. Even though some of the principles that uphold the Constitution may have been subverted, they have not been abolished.

Then I read the words of FDR at his 1933 inaugural:

Recognition of the falsity of material wealth as the standard of success goes hand in hand with the abandonment of the false belief that public office and high political position are to be valued only by the standards of pride of place and personal profit; and there must be an end to a conduct in banking and in business which too often has given to a sacred trust the likeness of callous and selfish wrongdoing. Small wonder that confidence languishes, for it thrives only on honesty, on honor, on the sacredness of obligations, on faithful protection, on unselfish performance; without them it cannot live.[14]

Then I remember all that my parents, Karl and Dora, went through to make a home in their new golden land, on the West Side of Chicago in the United States of America, to give my brothers and me a shot at being the first generation to live the American dream.

Because I have watched our country renew itself through the Great Depression and the fighting of WWII, and through decades of social reform and economic expansion that gave Americans of humble origins like me a chance to take our places as productive and respected members of American society, I believe in our country's great capacity to renew itself in times of distress.

Lest I sound like too much of an idealist, I note that the zenith years of the American dream did not yield absolute opportunity. But the zenith years of the American dream did yield greater chances for mobility and a more open and level playing field. They yielded more accessible policy making and more concern for the people's interests. Relative to today, those zenith years yielded better times for more Americans.

Now as then, however, I believe in Americans' ability to marshal our collective ingenuity and determination in order to turn tough times around.

Even today, with our American dream in peril, I continue to believe that our country has the best political system ever created in the history of humankind. We have seen how good it can be when we follow the principles according to which it was created. Now we are witnessing the terrible consequences of deserting those principles.

Unless we the people rise up once again and take control of our government and economy, this marvelous system may vanish. However, if our national conversation leads us to the knowledge that the power of change is still within our grasp – and to the knowledge that we *are* able to set things right – then we can act.

And I hope that we will act. I hope we will act so that my grandchildren will have the same freedoms and opportunities I had. So they will have the best education available. So their lives will be at least as comfortable as the life that I have had and even more fulfilling.

So that they will carry forward the same spirit of my father, who would often say:

"In America, anything is possible."

Chapter 1

[1] Wikipedia. "American Dream." Retrieved November 2011 at http://en.wikipedia.org/wiki/American_dream.

[2] Center for Responsive Politics. "Lobbying/Ranked Sectors." Washington, DC. Retrieved December 2011 at http://www.opensecrets.org/lobby/top.php?indexType=c.

[3] Eisenhower, Dwight D. "The Chance for Peace." April 16, 1953, Washington, DC. Retrieved January 2012 at http://www.edchange.org/multicultural/speeches/ike_chance_for_peace.html.

[4] U.S. Department of Defense. 2010. "Base Structure Report/Fiscal Year 2011 Baseline" (p. DoD-7). Retrieved November 2011 at http://www.acq.osd.mil/ie/download/bsr/bsr2011baseline.pdf.

[5] Wikipedia. "Military of the European Union." Retrieved November 2011 at http://en.wikipedia.org/wiki/Military_of_the_European_Union#Defence_Spending. See also Stockholm International Peace Research Institute (SIPRI), http://milexdata.sipri.org/.

[6] Shah, Anup. "World Military Spending." *Global Issues*, May 2, 2011. Retrieved November 2011 at http://www.globalissues.org/article/75/world-military-spending#WorldMilitarySpending

[7] Ibid.

[8] Saez, Emmanuel. "Striking it Richer: The Evolution of Top Incomes in the United States" (Figure 2: Decomposing the Top Decile US Income Share into 3 Groups, 1913-2008). July 17, 2010. Retrieved November 2011 at http://elsa.berkeley.edu/~saez/saez-UStopincomes-2008.pdf.

[9] U.S. Census Bureau. "Income, Poverty and Health Insurance Coverage in the United States: 2010." Sept. 13, 2011. Retrieved November 2011 at http://www.census.gov/newsroom/releases/archives/income_wealth/cb11-157.html

Chapter 2

[1] Fry, R., Cohn, D., Livingston, G. and Taylor, P. "The Rising Age Gap in Economic Well-Being: The Old Prosper Relative to the Young." Pew Social & Demographic Trends/Pew Research Center, Washington D.C. Nov. 7, 2011. Retrieved November 2011 at http://www.pewsocialtrends.org/2011/11/07/the-rising-age-gap-in-economic-well-being/.

[2] Ibid.

[3] Brill, Steven. "Government for Sale: How lobbyists shaped the financial reform bill." *Time* magazine, July 1, 2010.

[4] Bailey, Holly. "2010 campaigns cost $4 billion, and other fun election facts." Yahoo! News/*The Upshot*, Nov. 5, 2010. Retrieved November 2011 at http://news.yahoo.com/blogs/upshot/2010-campaigns-cost-4-billion-other-fun-election.html.

[5] "The Power of Money: The Ethics of Campaign Finance Reform." Markkula Center for Applied Ethics, Santa Clara University (undated). Retrieved November 2011 at http://www.scu.edu/ethics/publications/iie/v3n2/money.html

[6] Cummings, Jeanne. "2008 campaign costliest in U.S. history." *Politico*, Nov. 5, 2008. Retrieved November 2011 at http://dyn.politico.com/printstory.cfm?uuid=6A977A30-18FE-70B2-A893E630C5C38C0A.

[7] Froomkin, Dan. "Big Money – The Cost of Winning." *The Washington Post*, (updated) Sept. 4, 1998.

[8] Overby, Peter. "Where the Millions Go in a Presidential Campaign." National Public Radio, Feb. 13, 2007. Retrieved November 2011 at http://www.npr.org/templates/story/story.php?storyId=7386186.

[9] Brill. *Time*, July 2010.

[10] Ibid.

[11] Lichtblau, Eric. "Obama Backers Tied to Lobbies Raise Millions." *The New York Times*, Oct. 27, 2011.

[12] Overby, NPR, February 2007.

[13] Brill. *Time*, July 2010.

[14] Ibid.

[15] Center for Responsive Politics. "Lobbying Database." Washington, DC. Retrieved November 2011 at http://www.opensecrets.org/lobby/index.php.

[16] Brill. *Time*, July 2010.

[17] U.S. Supreme Court. *Citizens United v. Federal Election Commission*. Decided Jan. 21, 2010. Retrieved December 2011 at http://www.supremecourt.gov/opinions/09pdf/08-205.pdf.

[18] Center for Responsive Politics. "Sector Totals, 2011-2012." Washington, DC. Retrieved November 2011 at http://www.opensecrets.org/industries/index.php.

[19] Kang, Michael S. "After *Citizens United*." *Indiana Law Review*, 44:243, 2010. 243-254.

[20] Gilpatrick, Breanne. "Removing Corporate Campaign Finance Restrictions in *Citizens United v. Federal Election Commission*, 130 S. Ct. 876 (2010)." *Harvard Journal of Law & Public Policy*, 34:1, Winter 2011. 405-420.

[21] "National Voter Turnout in Federal Elections: 1960-2010." *Infoplease.* http://www.infoplease.com/ipa/A0781453.html.

Chapter 3

[1] Kennedy, David M. "What the New Deal Did." *Political Science Quarterly*. 124:2, 2009. 257-8.

[2] Wikipedia. "Freddie Mac." Retrieved November 2011 at http://en.wikipedia.org/wiki/Freddie_Mac.

[3] Kennedy, 258-9.

[4] Yeaman, Helena. "The Bipartisan Roots of the Financial Crisis." *Political Science Quarterly*. 124:4, 2009-10. 681-99.

[5] Ibid, 683-4.

[6] Ibid, 684.

[7] Ibid, 686-7.

[8] Ibid, 688.

[9] Ibid, 689.

[10] Canova, Timothy A. "Legacy of the Clinton Bubble," *Dissent*. Summer 2008, p. 43.

[11] Yeaman, 691-92.

[12] Ibid, 693.

[13] Merkley, Jeff and Levin, Carl. "Policy Essay: The Dodd-Frank Act Restrictions on Proprietary Trading and Conflicts of Interest: New Tools to Address Evolving Threats." *Harvard Journal on Legislation*. 48:2, 2011. 527.

[14] Mracek, Karen and Beaumont, Thomas. "Goldman reveals where bailout cash went." *USA Today,* July 26, 2010.

[15] Wikipedia. "Morgan Stanley." Retrieved November 2011 at http://en.wikipedia.org/wiki/Morgan_Stanley.

[16] Isidore, Chris. "Cost of Fannie & Freddie bailouts trimmed." *CNNMoney*, Nov 7, 2011. Retrieved November 2011 at http://money.cnn.com/2011/10/27/news/companies/fannie_freddie_bailout/index.htm.

[17] Stiglitz, Joseph. "Capitalist Fools." *Vanity Fair*, January 2009.

[18] "25 People to Blame for the Financial Crisis: The good intentions, bad managers and greed behind the meltdown." *Time.com*, Feb. 12, 2009. Retrieved November 2011 at http://www.time.com/time/specials/packages/completelist/0,29569,1877351,00.html.

[19] "25 People to Blame for the Financial Crisis: The good intentions, bad managers and greed behind the meltdown/Phil Gramm." *Time.com*, Feb. 12, 2009. Retrieved November 2011 at http://www.time.com/time/specials/packages/article/0,28804,1877351_1877350_1877330,00.html

[20] Corn, David. "Foreclosure Phil." *Mother Jones*, July/August 2008.

[21] "Blind Faith: How Deregulation and Enron's Influence Over Government Looted Billions from Americans." Public Citizen,

December 2001. Retrieved November 2011 at http://www.citizen.org/cmep/article_redirect.cfm?ID=7104.

[22] Herbert, Bob. "Enron and the Gramms." *The New York Times*, Jan. 17, 2002.

[23] Larsen, Jonathan, and Olbermann, Keith. "McCain economic policy shaped by lobbyist." *MSNBC.com*, May 27, 2008. Retrieved November 2011 at http://www.msnbc.msn.com/id/24844889/ns/msnbc_tv-countdown_with_keith_olbermann/t/mccain-economic-policy-shaped-lobbyist/

[24] "Wealth Management Americas/Revitalizing America: Senator Phil Gramm Vice Chairman, UBS Investment Bank." *UBS.com* (undated). Retrieved November 2011 at http://financialservicesinc.ubs.com/revitalizingamerica/SenatorPhilGramm.htm.l

[25] Merkley and Levin, 2011, p. 515.

[26] Wikipedia. "Volcker Rule." Retrieved November 2011 at http://en.wikipedia.org/wiki/Volcker_rule.

[27] Brill. *Time,* July 2010.

[28] Wikipedia. "Dodd–Frank Wall Street Reform and Consumer Protection Act." Retrieved November 2011 at http://en.wikipedia.org/wiki/Dodd-Frank_Wall_Street_Reform_and_Consumer_Protection_Act.

[29] Kaptur, Marcy. "Standing Up To Wall Street Greed." Retrieved November 2011 at http://www.kaptur.house.gov/index.php?option=com_content&task=view&id=637.

[30] Hoenig, Thomas. "Do SIFIS Have a Future?" Address to the Pew Financial Reform Project and New York University Stern School of Business "Dodd-Frank One Year On" conference in Washington, DC, June 27, 2011. Transcript retrieved November 2011 at http://www.kansascityfed.org/publicat/speeches/Hoenig-NYUPewConference-06-27-11.pdf.

[31] Reckard, E. Scott. "Federal Housing Finance Agency sues 17 banks over mortgage bonds." *Los Angeles Times*, Sept. 2, 2011. See also "FHFA Sues 17 Firms to Recover Losses to Fannie Mae and Freddie Mac" (press release). Federal Housing Finance Agency, Washington, DC. Sept. 2, 2011. Retrieved November 2011 at http://www.fhfa.gov/webfiles/22599/PLSLitigation_final_090211.pdf.

[32] Katz, Basil. "SEC sues former top execs at Fannie, Freddie." Reuters, Dec. 16, 2011.

[33] "Rod, meet Aaron" (editorial). *Chicago Tribune*, May 26, 2005.

[34] Miller, Rich. "Joe Berrios' odd press release." *The Capitol Fax Blog*, May 26, 2010. Retrieved November 2011 at http://thecapitolfaxblog.com/2010/05/26/joe-berrios-odd-press-release/.

[35] "No, thank you" (editorial). *Chicago Tribune*, May 27, 2010.

[36] Goldsborough, Bob. "Video gaming banned in unincorporated DuPage." *Chicago Tribune*, Aug. 11, 2009.

[37] Tarkov, Anna. "Evanston votes down video gambling." *Chicago Tribune*, Sept. 14, 2009.

[38] Goldsborough, *Chicago Tribune*, 2009.

[39] O'Shea, Gene. "Status of videogaming bans and communities that are considered bans" (memo). Illinois Gaming Board, Sept. 17, 2010.

[40] "Video poker extortion" (editorial). *Chicago Tribune,* Feb. 11, 2010.

[41] Ibid.

[42] Kidwell, David, and Long, Ray. "Regulators wince as video gambling bill advances." *Chicago Tribune*, May 24, 2010.

[43] "Why would we cut the mob in?" (editorial) *Chicago Sun-Times*, Aug. 3, 2010.

[44] "The bad guys won" (editorial). *Chicago Tribune*, Aug. 4, 2010.

[45] Warren, James. "In Turning to Video Gaming, the State Chases Fool's Gold." *Chicago News Cooperative*, Dec. 18, 2009. Retrieved November 2011 at http://www.chicagonewscoop.org/in-turning-to-video-gaming-the-state-chases-fool%e2%80%99s-gold/. Also published in *The New York Times* (under the same headline) on Dec. 18, 2009.

[46] U.S. Bureau of Labor Statistics, Jan. 17, 2012. Retrieved February 2012 at http://www.google.com/publicdata/explore?ds=z1ebjpgk2654c1_&met_y=unemployment_rate&idim=state:ST170000&fdim_y=seasonality:S&dl=en&hl=en&q=illinois+unemployment+rates.

[47] "Quinn signs tax hike into law." *Chicago Tribune*, Jan. 13, 2011.

[48] Bergen, Kathy. "Money woes, pension funding put Illinois in top 5 for per capita debt burden." *Chicago Tribune*, Jan. 28, 2011.

[49] Reynolds, Dean. "Illinois Income Tax Plan Draws Ire." CBS News, Jan. 14, 2011.

[50] "State of Illinois Enacted Budget FY2012: A Review of the Operating and Capital Budgets Enacted for the Current Fiscal Year." The Institute for Illinois' Fiscal Sustainability at the Civic Federation,

Chicago. Sept. 26, 2011. Retrieved November 2011 at http://www.civicfed.org/sites/default/files/State%20of%20Illinois%20Enacted%20Budget%20FY2012.pdf.

[51] Long, Ray; Pearson, Rick; and Garcia, Monique. "House bets on gambling boom, Chicago casino." *Chicago Tribune*, May 30, 2011.

[52] Spielman, Fran. "Video poker supporters trying to avoid raw deal; Backers say lifting city ban would save 130,000 jobs." *Chicago Sun-Times*, April 27, 2010.

[53] "Make them start over, Governor" (editorial). *Chicago Tribune*, June 18, 2011.

[54] "Gamblers and Illinois" (editorial). *Chicago Tribune*, Oct. 26, 2011.

[55] Pearson, Rick, and Garia, Monique. "Quinn report challenges revenue figure touted by backers of gambling expansion." *Chicago Tribune*, Nov. 22, 2011. See also "Illinois Statewide Gaming Market Assessment and Gaming Tax Analysis: Alternative Scenarios." Prepared for the Office of Governor Quinn by The Innovation Group, New Orleans, November 2011.

[56] "Quinn's opposition to casino bill is a gamble" (editorial). *Chicago Sun-Times*, Nov. 22, 2011.

[57] Ryan, Joseph and Ruthhart, Bill. "Gambling interests cover their bets with campaign contributions." *Chicago Tribune*, July 24, 2011.

[58] Ibid.

Chapter 4

[1] Applebaum, Binyamin. "Fed Chief Describes Consumers as Too Bleak." *The New York Times*, Sept. 8, 2011.

[2] Crutsinger, Martin. "S&P officials defend US credit downgrade." *Associated Press*, Aug. 6, 2011.

[3] Wagner, Daniel and Kravitz, Derek. "S&P downgrades Fannie and Freddie, US-backed debt." *Associated Press*, Aug. 8, 2011.

[4] Kuhnhenn, Jim. "Shutdown avoided, White House, Congress cheer deal." *Associated Press*, April 9, 2011.

[5] Calmes, Jackie. "Party Gridlock in Washington Feeds Fear of a Debt Crisis." *The New York Times*, Feb. 16, 2010.

[6] Smith, Adam C. "Michele Bachmann rally draws over 1,000 in Sarasota, but some prefer Rick Perry." *St. Petersburg Times*, Aug. 29, 2011.

Chapter 5

[1] Wikipedia. "Tower of Babel." Retrieved November 2011 at http://en.wikipedia.org/wiki/Tower_of_babel.

[2] Cassata, Donna. "Tea partiers say defense in mix for budget cuts." *Associated Press*, Jan. 23, 2011.

[3] Kennedy, *Political Science Quarterly*, 2009. p. 252.

[4] Frum, David. "Incredible Shrinking Workers' Income." *Frum Forum*, June 12, 2011. Retrieved November 2011 at http://www.frumforum.com/incredible-shrinking-workers-income. See also Roth, Zachary. "Workers' share of national income plummets to record low." Yahoo! News/*The Lookout*, June 14, 2011. Retrieved November 2011 at http://news.yahoo.com/blogs/lookout/workers-share-national-income-plummets-record-low-163749508.html.

[5] Ibid.

[6] Rapier, Robert. "Five myths about gas prices." *The Washington Post*, March 24, 2011.

[7] Froomkin, Dan. "Your Pain, Their Gain: How High Gas Prices Impoverish the Many While Enriching the Few." *The Huffington Post*, April 20, 2011. Retrieved November 2011 at http://www.huffingtonpost.com/2011/04/29/gas-prices-your-pain-their-gain_n_855673.html?view=print&comm_ref=false.

[8] Ibid.

[9] "Oil Price History and Analysis." WTRG Economics. Retrieved November 2011 at http://www.wtrg.com/prices.htm.

[10] Wikipedia. "Chicago Skyway." Retrieved November 2011 at http://en.wikipedia.org/wiki/Chicago_Skyway.

[11] The Coffee Party USA. http://www.coffeepartyusa.com/.

[12] Whitlock, Craig. "Pentagon to cut spending by $78 billion, reduce troop strength." *The Washington Post*, Jan. 7, 2011.

[13] "Text of President Obama's Tucson Memorial Speech." CBS News, Jan. 12, 2011. Retrieved November 2011 at http://www.cbsnews.com/8301-503544_162-20028366-503544.html.

[14] National Archives. "Teaching with Documents: FDR's First Inaugural Address." Document PDF pp. 3-4. Retrieved November 2011 at http://www.archives.gov/education/lessons/fdr-inaugural/.

www.ingramcontent.com/pod-product-compliance
Lightning Source LLC
Chambersburg PA
CBHW032106090426
42743CB00007B/258